best-ever

exciting recipes for every occasion

CHICKEN

best-ever

exciting recipes for every occasion

CHICKEN

contributing editor:
LINDA FRASER

HERMES
HOUSE

This edition published in 2004 by Hermes House

Hermes House is an imprint of Anness Publishing Limited
Hermes House, 88–89 Blackfriars Road, London SE1 8HA
tel. 020 7401 2077; fax. 020 7633 9499; info@anness.com

A CIP catalogue record for this book is available from the British Library.

Publisher: Joanna Lorenz
Cookery Editor: Rosemary Wilkinson
Copy Editor: Rosie Hankin
Designer: Bill Mason
Recipes: Catherine Atkinson, Alex Barker, Carla Capalbo, Maxine Clark, Andi Clevely, Christine France, Carole Handslip,
Sarah Gates, Shirley Gill, Norma MacMillan, Sue Maggs, Katherine Richmond,
Jenny Stacey, Ruby Le Bois, Liz Trigg, Hilaire Walden, Laura Washburn, Steven Wheeler
Photographers: Karl Adamson, Edward Allwright, Steve Baxter, James Duncan, John Freeman,
Michelle Garrett, Amanda Heywood, Don Last
Stylists: Madeleine Brehaut, Hilary Guy, Blake Minton, Kirsty Rawlings, Fiona Tillett
Food for Photography: Marilyn Forbes, Carole Handslip, Jane Hartshorn, Cara Hobday,
Beverly LeBlanc, Wendy Lee, Lucie McKelvie, Jenny Shapter, Elizabeth Silver, Jane Stevenson,
Liz Trigg, Elizabeth Wolf-Cohen
Illustrator: Anna Koska
1 3 5 7 9 10 8 6 4 2

Front cover shows Chicken and Mushroom Pie, for recipe see page 206.
Previously published as *Best-Ever Chicken*

NOTES
For all recipes, quantities are given in both metric and imperial measures and,
where appropriate, measures are also given in standard cups and spoons.
Follow one set, but not a mixture, because they are not interchangeable.
Standard spoon and cup measures are level.
1 tsp = 5ml, 1 tbsp = 15ml, 1 cup = 250ml/8fl oz
Australian standard tablespoons are 20ml. Australian readers should use 3 tsp in place of 1 tbsp for
measuring small quantities of gelatine, cornflour, salt, etc.
Medium eggs are used unless otherwise stated.

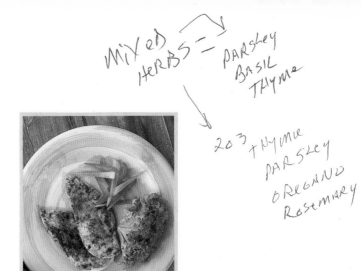

CONTENTS

Introduction

Chicken is popular with children and adults alike. It is versatile and economical, and can be cooked with a wide variety of ingredients and flavors. It is low in fat and quick to cook, with very little wastage.

Chicken can be bought in many forms: whole, quartered or cut into thighs, drumsticks, breasts and wings, with or without bones and skin, which makes preparation very easy. Ground chicken can be found at some large supermarkets, but the skinned flesh can be ground quickly in a food processor. Although it is convenient to buy portions individually packed, it is expensive. It is much cheaper to buy a whole chicken and prepare it yourself and cheaper still to buy a frozen chicken and defrost it thoroughly before using. To get the best results from a frozen bird, allow it to thaw slowly in a cool place overnight or until completely defrosted. Many types of chicken are available, such as free-range and corn-fed (with yellow skin) and all are full of flavor. Some have added herbs and flavorings, and others are self-basting with either butter or olive oil injected into the flesh. This helps to keep the flesh succulent. Rock Cornish hens are the smallest domestic birds available; they weigh from ¾ to 2 pounds. Sometimes found fresh, they are always available frozen. Chickens weigh from 2-6 pounds, and turkey up to 25 or more, so there's a bird to suit every family and occasion.

The recipes in this book are mostly based on a family of four people, but they can be easily halved for two or doubled for eight. There are chapters on soups, salads and pies as well as one pot meals, midweek meals and hot and spicy dishes to provide you with a best-ever chicken meal for every occasion.

Choosing a Chicken

A fresh chicken should have a plump breast and the skin should be creamy in color. The tip of the breast bone should be pliable.

A bird's dressed weight is taken after plucking and drawing and may include the giblets (neck, gizzard, heart and liver). A frozen chicken must be thawed slowly in the fridge or a cool room. Never put it in hot water, as this will toughen the flesh and is dangerous as it allows bacteria to multiply.

Rock Cornish hens
These are four to six weeks old and weigh 1–1¼ pounds. One is enough for one person.

Broiling chickens
These are eight to ten weeks old and weigh 1¾–2 pounds. One will serve two people. Poussins are best roasted, broiled or pot-roasted.

Roasters
These birds are about six to twelve months old and weigh 3–6 pounds. One will feed a family.

Boiling fowl
These are about twelve months old and over and weigh between 4–6 pounds. They require long, slow cooking, around 2–3 hours, to make them tender.

Corn-fed chickens
These are free-range birds, and are generally more expensive. They usually weigh 2½–3 pounds.

Frying chickens
These birds are about three months old and weigh 2–3 pounds. One will serve three to four people.

Cuts of Chicken

Chicken pieces are available pre-packaged in various forms. If you do not want to buy a whole bird, you can make your choice from the many cuts on the market.

Some cooking methods are especially suited to specific cuts of poultry.

Liver
This makes a wonderful addition to pâtés or to salads.

Drumstick
The drumstick is a firm favorite for barbecuing or frying, either in batter or rolled in breadcrumbs.

Wing
The wing does not supply much meat, and is often barbecued or fried.

Skinless boneless thigh
This makes tasks such as stuffing and rolling much quicker, as it is already skinned and dis-jointed.

Thigh
The thigh is suitable for casseroling and other slow-cooking methods.

Breast
The tender white meat can be simply cooked in butter, or can be stuffed for extra flavor.

Ground chicken
This is not as strongly flavored as, say, ground beef, but it may be used as a substitute in some recipes.

Leg
This comprises the drumstick and thigh. Large pieces with bones, such as this, are suitable for slow-cooking, such as casseroling or poaching.

Trussing Poultry

Trussing holds a bird together during cooking so that it keeps a neat, attractive shape. If the bird is stuffed, trussing prevents the stuffing from falling out. You can truss with strong string or poultry skewers.

An alternative to the method shown here is to use a long trussing needle and fine cotton string: make two passes, in alternate directions, through the body at the open end, from wing to wing, and tie. Then pass the needle through the pope's nose and tie the string around the ends of the drumsticks.

Remove trussing before serving.

1 For an unstuffed bird: set it breast down and pull the neck skin over the neck opening. Turn the bird breast up and fold the wing tips back, over the skin, to secure behind the shoulders.

2 Press the legs down firmly and into the breast. If there is a band of skin across the pope's nose, fold back the ends of the drumsticks and tuck them under the skin.

3 Otherwise, cross the knuckle ends of the drumsticks or bring them tightly together. Loop a length of string several times around the drumstick ends, tie a knot and trim off excess string.

4 For a stuffed bird: fold the wing tips back as above. After stuffing the neck end, fold the flap of skin over the opening and secure it with a skewer, then fold over the wing tips.

5 Put any stuffing or flavorings (herbs, lemon halves, apple quarters and so on) in the body cavity, then secure the ends of the drumsticks as above, tying in the pope's nose, too.

6 Or, the cavity opening can be closed with skewers: insert two or more skewers across the opening, threading them through the skin several times.

7 Lace the skewers together with string. Tie the drumsticks together over the skewers.

STUFFING TIPS

Only use stuffing that is cool, not hot or chilled. Pack it loosely in the bird and cook any leftovers separately. Stuff poultry just before cooking. Do not stuff the body cavity of a large bird because this could inhibit heat penetration, and thus harmful bacteria may not be destroyed.

Roasting Poultry

Where would family gatherings be without the time-honored roast bird? Beyond the favorite chicken, all types of poultry can be roasted – from Rock Cornish hens to large turkeys. However, older, tougher birds are better pot-roasted.

1 Wipe the bird inside and out with damp paper towels, stuff, if desired and truss it. Spread the breast of chicken with soft butter or oil; bard a lean game bird; prick the skin of duck or goose.

2 Set the bird breast up on a rack in a small roasting pan or shallow baking dish. If you are roasting a lean game bird, set the bird in the pan breast down.

3 Roast the bird, basting every 10 minutes after the first 30 minutes with the juices and fat in the pan. If browning too quickly, cover with foil.

4 Put the bird on a carving board and let it rest for at least 15 minutes before serving. Meanwhile make a simple sauce or gravy with the juices in the pan.

SIMPLE ROAST CHICKEN

Squeeze the juice from a halved lemon over a 3–3^1/$_2$-pound chicken, then push the lemon halves into the body cavity. Smear 1 tablespoon softened butter over the breast. Roast in a 375°F oven for about 1^1/$_4$ hours. Skim all fat from the roasting juices, then add ^{1}/$_2$ cup water and bring to a boil, stirring well to mix in the browned bits. Season with salt and pepper, and serve this sauce with the chicken. Serves 4.

ROASTING TIMES FOR POULTRY

Note: Cooking times given here are for unstuffed birds.
For stuffed birds, add 20 minutes to the total roasting time.

ROCK CORNISH HEN	1–1^1/$_2$ pounds	1–1^1/$_4$ hours at 350°F
CHICKEN	2^1/$_2$–3 pounds	1–1^1/$_4$ hours at 375°F
	3^1/$_2$–4 pounds	1^1/$_4$–2 hours at 375°F
	4^1/$_2$–5 pounds	1^1/$_2$–2 hours at 375°F
	5–6 pounds	1^3/$_4$–2^1/$_2$ hours at 375°F
DUCK	3–5 pounds	1^3/$_4$–2^1/$_4$ hours at 400°F
GOOSE	8–10 pounds	2^1/$_2$–3 hours at 350°F
	10–12 pounds	3–3^1/$_2$ hours at 350°F
TURKEY	6–8 pounds	3–3^1/$_2$ hours at 325°F
(whole bird)	8–12 pounds	3–4 hours at 325°F
	12–16 pounds	4–5 hours at 325°F
TURKEY	4–6 pounds	1^1/$_2$–2^1/$_4$ hours at 325°F
(whole breast)	6–8 pounds	2^1/$_4$–3^1/$_4$ hours at 325°F

PROTECT & FLAVOR

Before roasting, loosen the skin on the breast by gently easing it away from the flesh with your fingers. Press in softened butter – mixed with herbs or garlic for extra flavor – and smooth back the skin. To bard poultry, cover the breast with slices of bacon before roasting.

Cutting Up Poultry

Although chickens and other poultry are sold already cut into halves, quarters, breasts, thighs and drumsticks, sometimes it makes sense to buy a whole bird and to do the job yourself. That way you can prepare four larger pieces or eight smaller ones, depending on the recipe, and you can cut the pieces so the backbone and other bony bits (which can be saved for stock) are not included. Also, a whole bird is cheaper to buy than pieces.

A sharp knife and sturdy kitchen scissors or poultry shears make the job of cutting up poultry very easy.

1 With the sharp knife, cut through the skin on one side of the body down to where the thigh joins the body. Bend the leg out away from the body and twist it to break the ball and socket joint.

2 Hold the leg out away from the body and cut through the ball and socket joint, taking the "oyster meat" from the backbone with the leg. Repeat on the other side.

3 To separate the breast from the back, cut through the flap of skin just below the rib cage, cutting towards the neck. Pull the breast and back apart, cutting through the joints that connect them. Reserve the back for stock.

4 Turn the whole breast over, skin side down. Take one side of the breast in each hand and bend back firmly so the breastbone pops free. Loosen the bone on both sides with your fingers and, using a knife to help, remove it.

5 Cut the breast lengthwise in half, cutting through the wishbone. You now have 2 breasts with wings attached and 2 leg portions.

6 For 8 pieces, cut each breast in half at an angle so that some breast is included with each wing. Trim off any protruding bones.

7 With the knife, cut each leg portion through the ball and socket joint to separate the thigh and drumstick.

Boning a Chicken

For the purpose of stuffing, and to make carving simple, it is essential to bone a chicken. Use a sharp knife with a short blade. Work in short, scraping movements, keeping the knife against the bone at all times, to leave the carcass clean.

1 Remove any trussing string. Cut off the wing tips (pinions) and discard. With a short-bladed, sharp knife, cut the skin along the underside (backbone) of the chicken. Carefully work the skin and flesh away from the carcass with the knife until the leg joints are exposed.

2 Cut the sinew between the ball and socket joints. This sinew joins the thigh bones and wings to the carcass.

3 Holding the rib cage away from the chicken body, carefully scrape the breastbone clean and cut the carcass away from the skin. Take great care not to cut through the skin, or the stuffing will burst out of the hole.

4 Take hold of the thigh bone in one hand, and with the knife scrape the flesh down the bone to the next joint.

5 Cut around the joint and continue cleaning the drumstick until the whole leg bone is free. Repeat with the other leg and both the wings. Lay the chicken flat and turn the flesh of the legs and wings inside the chicken. Flatten the flesh neatly so the bird is ready to stuff.

HANDLING RAW POULTRY

Raw poultry may harbor harmful organisms, such as salmonella bacteria, so it is vital to take care in its preparation. Always wash your hands, cutting board, knife and poultry shears in hot soapy water before and after handling poultry. If possible, use a cutting board that can be washed at a high temperature in a dishwasher, and always keep a cutting board just for the preparation of raw poultry. Thaw frozen poultry completely before cooking.

Butterflying Poultry

Whole chickens, Rock Cornish hens, guinea fowl and game birds can be split in half and opened flat like a book to resemble the wings of a butterfly. They will then cook evenly under the broiler or on a grill. A heavy knife can be used to split the bird, but sturdy kitchen scissors or poultry shears are easier to handle.

1 Set the bird breast down. Cut through the skin and rib cage along one side of the backbone, working from the tail end to the neck. Repeat on the other side of the backbone to cut it free. Keep the backbone for stock, if desired.

2 Turn the bird breast up. With the heel of your hand, press firmly on the breastbone to break it and flatten the breast.

3 Fold the wing tips back behind the shoulders. Thread a long metal skewer through one wing and the top of the breast and out through the other wing.

4 Thread a second skewer through the thighs and bottom of the breast. These skewers will keep the bird flat during cooking and will make it easy to turn over.

TESTING POULTRY

~

Overcooked poultry is dry, tough and tasteless, so knowing when a bird is done is crucial. The most reliable test for a whole bird is to insert a meat thermometer deep into the thigh meat (the internal temperature should be 175°F). Without a thermometer, you can test by piercing the thigh with a skewer or the tip of a knife; the juices that run out should be clear, not pink. Or, lift the bird with a long two-pronged fork and tilt it so you can check the color of the juices that run out of the cavity into the roasting pan. Pieces of poultry, particularly breasts, can be tested by pressing them with a finger; the meat should be firm but still slightly springy.

BROILING TIMES FOR POULTRY

Note: Cook 4–6 inches from the heat; thinner pieces, less than 1 inch nearer the heat.
If the poultry seems to be browning too quickly, turn down the heat slightly.

ROCK CORNISH HEN, BUTTERFLIED	20–25 minutes
CHICKEN, BROILER OR FRYER, SPLIT IN HALF OR BUTTERFLIED	25–30 minutes
ROASTING CHICKEN, SPLIT IN HALF OR BUTTERFLIED	30–40 minutes
CHICKEN BREAST, DRUMSTICK, THIGH	30–35 minutes
SKINLESS BONELESS CHICKEN BREAST	10–12 minutes
BONELESS DUCK BREAST	10–12 minutes

Making Poultry Stock

A good homemade poultry stock is invaluable in the kitchen. It is simple and economical to make, and can be stored in the freezer for up to 6 months. If poultry giblets are available, add them (except the livers) with the wings.

INGREDIENTS

Makes about 10 cups

$2^1/_2$–3 pounds poultry wings, backs and necks (chicken, turkey, etc)

2 onions, unpeeled, quartered

7 pints cold water

2 carrots, coarsely chopped

2 celery stalks, with leaves if possible, coarsely chopped

a small handful of fresh parsley

a few fresh thyme sprigs or

$^3/_4$ teaspoon dried thyme

1 or 2 bay leaves

10 black peppercorns, lightly crushed

FRUGAL STOCK
❧

Stock can be made from the bones and carcasses of roasted poultry, cooked with vegetables and flavorings. Save the carcasses in a plastic bag in the freezer until you have three or four, then make stock. It may not have quite as rich a flavor as stock made from a whole bird or fresh wings, backs and necks, but it will still taste fresher and less salty than stock made from a commercial cube.

---

1 Combine the poultry wings, backs and necks and the onions in a stockpot. Cook over moderate heat until the poultry and onion pieces are lightly browned, stirring from time to time so they color evenly.

3 Add the remaining ingredients. Partially cover the stockpot and gently simmer the stock for about 3 hours.

5 When cold, carefully remove the layer of fat that will have settled on the surface.

2 Add the water and stir well to mix in the sediment on the bottom of the pot. Bring to a boil and skim off the impurities as they rise to the surface of the stock.

4 Strain the stock into a bowl and allow to cool, then refrigerate.

STOCK TIPS
❧

If desired, use a whole bird for making stock instead of wings, backs and necks. A boiling fowl, if available, will give wonderful flavor and provide meat to use in salads, sandwiches, soups and casseroles.

No salt is added to stock because as the stock reduces, the flavor becomes concentrated and the saltiness increases. Add salt to dishes which contain the stock.

Making Poultry Sautés

A sauté combines frying and braising, producing especially succulent results. It is a method suitable for pieces of poultry as well as for small whole birds such as quails and Rock Cornish hens.

As with frying, the poultry should be dried thoroughly with paper towels before cooking, to make sure that it browns quickly and evenly.

COUNTRY CHICKEN SAUTE

Cook 6 ounces chopped bacon in 2 teaspoons oil over moderately high heat until lightly colored. Remove bacon and reserve. Dredge a 3^1/$_2$-pound chicken, cut into eight pieces, in seasoned flour. Fry chicken pieces in the bacon fat until evenly browned. Add 3 tablespoons of dry white wine and 1 cup poultry stock. Bring to a boil and add 8 ounces quartered mushrooms sautéed in 1 tablespoon of butter and the reserved bacon. Cover and cook over low heat for 20–25 minutes, or until the chicken is tender.
Serves 4.

1 Heat a little oil, a mixture of oil and butter, or clarified butter in a heavy frying or sauté pan.

2 Add the poultry and fry over medium heat until it is golden brown, turning to color evenly.

3 Add any liquid and flavorings called for in the recipe. Bring to a boil, then cover and reduce the heat to medium low. Continue cooking gently until the poultry is done, turning the pieces or birds over once or twice.

4 If the recipe requires it remove the poultry from the pan and keep it warm while finishing the sauce. This can be as simple as boiling the cooking juices to reduce them or adding butter or cream for a richer result.

5 To thicken the cooking juices use equal weights of butter and flour mashed together. Use 1 ounce of this "beurre manié" to 1 cup liquid. Add small pieces gradually to the hot juices and whisk until mixture is smooth.

6 Another method of thickening cooking juices is to use cornstarch. Blend 2 teaspoons cornstarch with 1 tablespoon water and add to 1 cup juices. Boil, whisking, for 2–3 minutes, until the sauce is syrupy.

Frying Chicken

*Fried chicken is justifiably popular –
crisp and brown outside and tender
and juicy within. It's a quick and
easy cooking method that can be
applied to pieces of rabbit and hare
and small turkey joints, too.*

   *Dry the pieces thoroughly with
paper towels before frying. If they
are at all wet, they will not brown
properly. If the recipe suggests it,
lightly coat the pieces with egg and
crumbs or with a batter.*

SUCCULENT FRIED CHICKEN

Mix 1 cup milk with 1 beaten
egg in a shallow dish. On a sheet
of waxed paper combine 1¹/₄
cups all-purpose flour, 1 teaspoon paprika, and some salt
and pepper. One at a time, dip
eight chicken pieces in the egg
mixture and turn them to coat
all over. Then dip in the seasoned flour and shake off any
excess. Deep-fry for 25–30
minutes, turning the pieces so
they brown and cook evenly.
Drain on paper towels and
serve very hot.
Serves 4.

1 To pan-fry, heat oil, a mixture
of oil and butter, or clarified
butter in a large, heavy-bottomed
frying pan over medium heat.
When very hot, add the chicken
pieces, skin-side down.

3 To deep-fry, dip the pieces into
a mixture of milk and beaten
egg and coat lightly with seasoned
flour. Allow coating to set for
20 minutes before frying. (Or, dip
the pieces in batter before frying.)

5 With a spatula or tongs, lower
the chicken pieces into the oil,
a few at a time. Deep-fry, turning
during cooking, until they are
golden brown all over and cooked.

2 Fry until deep golden brown all
over, turning the pieces during
cooking. Fry until the pieces are
thoroughly cooked. Remove pieces
of breast before drumsticks and
thighs. Drain on paper towels.

4 Half fill a deep pan with
vegetable oil. Heat it to 365°F.
You can test the temperature with
a cube of bread; if it takes
50 seconds to brown, the oil is at
the right temperature.

6 Drain on paper towels and
serve hot. If you want to keep a
batch of fried chicken hot while
frying the rest, put it, uncovered,
into a low oven.

Poaching, Casseroling & Braising

SIMPLE CHICKEN STOCK

This all-purpose chicken stock may be used as the basis for a wonderful homemade soup.

1 Put the giblets (the neck, gizzard and heart, but not the liver, as it makes stock bitter), or the carcass from a cooked chicken, into a pan and just cover with cold water.

2 Add a quartered onion, carrot, bouquet garni (bay leaf, thyme and parsley) and a few peppercorns. Bring to a boil, cover and simmer gently for 1–2 hours.

3 Remove any scum that rises to the surface with a large slotted spoon. Alternatively, make the stock when you cook the chicken, by putting the giblets in the roasting pan around the chicken with the onion and herbs and just enough water to keep them from burning.

4 When the stock has cooled and set, carefully remove the fat from the surface with a spoon. Add salt to taste when using the stock.

POACHING

Poaching is a very gentle cooking method and produces stock for making a sauce afterwards.

1 Put the chicken into a flameproof casserole with a bouquet garni (bay leaf, thyme and parsley), carrot and onion.

2 Cover with water and add salt and peppercorns. Bring to a boil, cover and simmer for about 1½ hours, or until tender.

3 Cool in the liquid or lift out, shred, and combine with a white sauce.

BRAISING

This method can be used for whole chickens and pieces and is ideal for strongly-flavored meat.

1 Heat olive oil in a flameproof casserole and lightly fry a chicken or pieces until golden.

2 Remove the chicken and stir-fry 1 pound of diced vegetables (carrots, onions, celery and turnips), until soft.

3 Replace the chicken, cover tightly, and cook very slowly on the stovetop or in a preheated oven at 325°F, until tender.

CASSEROLING

This slow-cooking method is good for large chicken joints with bones, or more mature meat.

1 Heat olive oil in a flameproof casserole and brown the chicken joints.

2 Add some stock, wine or a mixture of both to a depth of 1 inch. Add seasonings and herbs, cover, and cook on the stovetop or in the oven, as for braising, for 1–1½ hours, or until tender.

3 Add a selection of lightly stir-fried vegetables such as baby onions, mushrooms, carrots and small new potatoes about halfway through the cooking time.

Five Stuffings for Chicken

BASIC HERB STUFFING

INGREDIENTS

1 small onion, finely chopped
1 tablespoon butter
2 cups fresh breadcrumbs
1 tablespoon chopped fresh parsley
1 teaspoon mixed dried herbs
1 egg, beaten
salt and black pepper

Cook the onion gently in the butter until tender. Allow to cool.

Add to the remaining ingredients and then mix thoroughly. Season well with salt and pepper.

VARIATIONS

Any of these ingredients may be added to the basic recipe to vary the flavor of the stuffing, depending on what you have in your fridge and cupboards at home.

1 celery stalk, finely chopped
1 small eating apple, diced
$1/2$ cup chopped walnuts
　or almonds
1 tablespoon raisins
$1/4$ cup chopped dried prunes
　or apricots
$2/3$ cup mushrooms, finely chopped
grated rind of $1/2$ orange or lemon
$1/2$ cup pine nuts
2 strips bacon, chopped

APRICOT AND ORANGE STUFFING

INGREDIENTS

1 tablespoon butter
1 small onion, finely chopped
2 cups fresh breadcrumbs
$1/4$ cup finely chopped dried
　apricots
grated rind of $1/2$ orange
1 small egg, beaten
1 tablespoon chopped fresh
　parsley
salt and black pepper

Heat the butter in a frying pan and cook the onion gently until tender.

Allow to cool slightly, and add to the rest of the ingredients. Mix until thoroughly combined and season with salt and pepper.

RAISIN AND NUT STUFFING

INGREDIENTS

2 cups fresh breadcrumbs
$1/3$ cup raisins
$1/2$ cup walnuts, almonds, pistachios or
　pine nuts
1 tablespoon chopped fresh
　parsley
1 teaspoon chopped mixed herbs
1 small egg, beaten
2 tablespoons melted butter
salt and black pepper

Mix all the ingredients together thoroughly. Season well with salt and pepper.

PARSLEY, LEMON AND THYME STUFFING

INGREDIENTS

2 cups fresh breadcrumbs
2 tablespoons butter
1 tablespoon chopped fresh parsley
$1/2$ teaspoon dried thyme
grated rind of $1/4$ lemon
1 strip lean bacon, chopped
1 small egg, beaten
salt and black pepper

Mix all the ingredients together to combine them thoroughly.

Parsley, Lemon and Thyme Stuffing

SAUSAGE STUFFING

INGREDIENTS

1 tablespoon butter
1 small onion, finely chopped
2 strips lean bacon, chopped
8 ounces sausage meat
$1/2$ teaspoon mixed dried herbs
salt and black pepper

Heat the butter in a frying pan and cook the onion until tender. Add the bacon and cook for 5 minutes, then allow to cool.

Add to the remaining ingredients and mix thoroughly.

Raisin and Nut Stuffing

SOUPS & APPETIZERS

Chicken and Lentil Soup

A chunky soup that makes a good lunchtime dish.

INGREDIENTS

Serves 4

2 tablespoons butter or margarine

1 large carrot, chopped

1 onion, chopped

1 leek, white part only, chopped

1 celery stalk, chopped

4 ounces mushrooms, chopped

3 tablespoons dry white wine

4 cups homemade or canned chicken
  stock

2 teaspoons dried thyme

1 bay leaf

$1/2$ cup brown or green lentils

8 ounces cooked chicken, diced

salt and black pepper

1 Melt the butter or margarine in a large saucepan. Add the carrot, onion, leek, celery and mushrooms. Cook for 3–5 minutes, until softened.

2 Stir in the wine and chicken stock. Bring to a boil and skim off any foam that rises to the surface. Add the thyme and bay leaf. Reduce the heat, cover, and simmer for 30 minutes.

3 Add the lentils and continue cooking, covered, for another 30–40 minutes, until they are just tender, stirring the soup from time to time.

4 Stir in the diced chicken and season to taste with salt and pepper. Cook until just heated through. Ladle the soup into bowls and serve hot.

Chicken Vermicelli Soup with Egg Shreds

This light soup can be put together in a matter of minutes and is full of flavor.

INGREDIENTS

Serves 4–6

3 jumbo eggs

2 tablespoons chopped cilantro
  or parsley

6¼ cups homemade or canned chicken
  stock

1 cup dried vermicelli or angel
  hair pasta

4 ounces cooked chicken breast, sliced

salt and pepper

1 First make the egg shreds.
Whisk the eggs together in a
small bowl and stir in the chopped
cilantro or parsley.

2 Heat a small nonstick frying
pan and pour in 2–3 tablespoons beaten egg, swirling to
cover the bottom evenly. Cook
until set. Repeat until all the
mixture is used up.

3 Roll each pancake up and slice
thinly into shreds. Set aside.

4 Bring the stock to a boil and
add the pasta, breaking it into
short lengths. Cook for 3–5
minutes, until the pasta is almost
tender, then add the chicken, salt
and pepper. Heat through for 2–3
minutes, then stir in the egg
shreds. Serve immediately.

Cream of Scallion Soup

A meltingly smooth soup of chicken stock, potato and scallions.

INGREDIENTS

Serves 4–6

2 tablespoons butter

1 small onion, chopped

5 ounces scallions, white parts only, chopped

8 ounces potato, peeled and chopped

$2^1/2$ cups homemade or canned chicken stock

$1^1/2$ cups light cream

salt and white pepper

2 tablespoons lemon juice

chopped scallions or chives, to garnish

1 Melt the butter in a saucepan and add all the onions. Cover and cook over very low heat for about 10 minutes, or until soft.

2 Add the potatoes and the stock. Bring to a boil, cover again, and simmer over medium low heat for 30 minutes. Cool slightly.

3 Purée the soup in a blender or food processor.

4 If serving the soup hot, pour it back into the pan. Add the cream and season. Reheat gently, stirring frequently. Stir in the lemon juice and garnish before serving.

Zucchini Soup with Small Pasta Shells

An attractive and refreshing soup which could be made using cucumber instead of zucchini.

INGREDIENTS

Serves 4–6

4 tablespoons olive or sunflower oil

2 medium onions, finely chopped

6¹/₄ cups homemade or canned chicken stock

2 pounds zucchini

1 cup small pasta for soup

fresh lemon juice

salt and pepper

2 tablespoons chopped fresh chervil

sour cream, to serve

1 Heat the oil in a large saucepan and add the onions. Cover and cook gently for about 20 minutes, until very soft but not colored, stirring occasionally.

2 Add the chicken stock and bring to a boil.

3 Meanwhile grate the zucchini and stir into the boiling stock with the pasta. Turn down the heat and simmer for 15 minutes, until the pasta is tender. Season to taste with lemon juice, salt and pepper.

4 Stir in the chervil and add a swirl of sour cream to serve.

Country Vegetable Soup

To stir things up, vary the vegetables according to the season.

INGREDIENTS

Serves 4

4 tablespoons butter

1 onion, chopped

2 leeks, sliced

2 celery stalks, sliced

2 carrots, sliced

2 small turnips, chopped

4 ripe tomatoes, peeled and chopped

4 cups homemade or canned
   chicken stock

bouquet garni

4 ounces green beans, chopped

salt and pepper

chopped herbs such as tarragon, thyme,
   chives and parsley, to garnish

1 Heat the butter in a large saucepan, add the onion and leeks and cook gently until soft but not colored.

2 Add the celery, carrots and turnips and cook for 3–4 minutes, stirring occasionally. Stir in the tomatoes and stock, add the bouquet garni and simmer for about 20 minutes.

3 Add the beans to the soup and cook until all the vegetables are tender. Season to taste and serve garnished with chopped herbs.

Split Pea and Bacon Soup

In England, another name for this soup is "London Particular," from the dense fogs for which the city used to be notorious. The fogs in turn were called "pea-soupers."

INGREDIENTS

Serves 4

1 tablespoon butter

4 ounces Canadian bacon, chopped

1 large onion, chopped

1 carrot, chopped

1 celery stalk, chopped

$1/2$ cup split peas

5 cups homemade or canned
   chicken stock

2 thick slices firm bread, buttered and
   without crusts

2 slices lean bacon

salt and pepper

1 Heat the butter in a saucepan, add the Canadian bacon and cook until the fat runs. Stir in the onion, carrot and celery and cook for 2–3 minutes.

2 Add the split peas and then the stock. Bring to a boil, stirring occasionally, then cover and simmer for 45–60 minutes.

3 Meanwhile, preheat the oven to 350°F and bake the bread on a baking sheet for about 20 minutes, until crisp and brown, then cut into cubes.

4 Broil the lean bacon until very crisp, then chop finely.

5 When the soup is ready, season to taste and serve hot with chopped bacon and croutons sprinkled on each portion.

Mulligatawny Soup

Mulligatawny (which means "pepper water") was introduced into England in the late eighteenth century, by members of the army and colonial service returning home from India.

INGREDIENTS

Serves 4

4 tablespoons butter or 4 tablespoons
    olive oil

2 large chicken joints, about
    12 ounces each

1 onion, chopped

1 carrot, chopped

1 small turnip, chopped

about 1 tablespoon curry powder, to taste

4 cloves

6 black peppercorns, lightly crushed

$^1/_4$ cup lentils

$3^3/_4$ cups homemade or canned
    chicken stock

$^1/_4$ cup golden raisins

salt and pepper

1 Melt the butter or heat the oil in a large saucepan and brown the chicken over brisk heat. Transfer the chicken onto a plate.

COOK'S TIP

Red split lentils will give the best color for this dish, although green or brown lentils could be used, if you prefer.

2 Add the onion, carrot and turnip to the pan and cook, stirring occasionally, until lightly colored. Stir in the curry powder, cloves and peppercorns and cook for 1–2 minutes. Add the lentils.

3 Pour in the stock and bring to a boil. Add the golden raisins and chicken and any juices from the plate. Cover and simmer gently for about $1^1/_4$ hours.

4 Remove the chicken from the pan and discard the skin and bones. Chop the flesh, return to the soup and reheat. Check and adjust the seasoning before serving the soup piping hot.

Thai Chicken Soup

This filling and tasty soup is very quick to prepare and cook.

INGREDIENTS

Serves 4

1 tablespoon vegetable oil

1 garlic clove, finely chopped

2 boned chicken breasts, about 6 ounces each, skinned and chopped

$^1/_2$ teaspoon ground turmeric

$^1/_4$ teaspoon hot chili powder

3 ounces creamed coconut

$3^3/_4$ cups hot homemade or canned chicken stock,

2 tablespoons lemon or lime juice

2 tablespoons crunchy peanut butter

1 cup thread egg noodles, broken into small pieces

1 tablespoon scallions, finely chopped

1 tablespoon chopped fresh cilantro

salt and black pepper

2 tablespoons dried coconut and $^1/_2$ fresh red chili, seeded and finely chopped, to garnish

1 Heat the oil in a large pan and fry the garlic for 1 minute, until lightly golden. Add the chicken and spices and stir-fry for another 3–4 minutes.

2 Crumble the creamed coconut into the hot chicken stock and stir until dissolved. Pour onto the chicken and add the lemon or lime juice, peanut butter and egg noodles.

3 Cover the pan and simmer for about 15 minutes.

4 Add the chopped scallions and cilantro, then season well and cook for another 5 minutes. Meanwhile, place the dried coconut and chili in a small frying pan and heat for 2–3 minutes, stirring frequently.

5 Serve the soup in bowls and sprinkle each one with some fried coconut and hot chili.

New England Spiced Pumpkin Soup

Pumpkin soup cooked with spices, brown sugar and orange juice.

INGREDIENTS

Serves 4

2 tablespoons butter

1 onion, finely chopped

1 small garlic clove, crushed

1 tablespoon all-purpose flour

pinch of grated nutmeg

$1/2$ teaspoon ground cinnamon

3 cups pumpkin, seeded,
    peeled and cubed

$2^1/2$ cups homemade or canned
    chicken stock

$2/3$ cup orange juice

1 teaspoon brown sugar

1 tablespoon vegetable oil

2 slices whole wheat bread without crusts

2 tablespoons sunflower seeds

1 Heat the butter in a large saucepan, add the onion and garlic and fry gently for 4–5 minutes, until softened. Stir in the flour, all the spices and the pumpkin,

2 Cover and cook gently for about 6 minutes, stirring occasionally.

3 Pour in the chicken stock and orange juice and add the brown sugar. Cover and bring to a boil, then reduce the heat and simmer for 20 minutes, until the pumpkin has softened.

4 Pour half of the mixture into a blender or food processor and process until smooth. Return the soup to the pan with the remaining chunky mixture. Season well and heat through, stirring.

5 Meanwhile, make the croutons. Heat the oil in a frying pan, cut the bread into cubes and fry gently until just beginning to brown. Add the sunflower seeds and fry for 1–2 minutes. Drain the croutons and sunflower seeds on paper towels.

6 Serve the soup hot with a few of the croutons and sunflower seeds sprinkled over the top. Serve the rest separately.

Green Pea and Mint Soup

This soup is equally delicious cold. Instead of reheating it after puréeing, let it cool and then chill lightly in the fridge. Stir in the swirl of cream just before serving.

INGREDIENTS

Serves 4

4 tablespoons butter

4 scallions, chopped

4 cups fresh or frozen peas

2^1/$_2$ cups homemade or canned chicken stock

2 large mint sprigs

2^1/$_2$ cups milk

pinch of sugar (optional)

salt and pepper

light cream, to serve

small mint sprigs, to garnish

1 Heat the butter in a large saucepan, add the scallions, and cook gently until softened but not colored.

FREEZER NOTE

The soup can be frozen for up to two months after step 2. Allow it to thaw in the fridge before puréeing and reheating.

2 Stir the peas into the pan, add the stock and mint and bring to a boil. Cover and simmer very gently for about 30 minutes for fresh peas, or 15 minutes if you are using frozen peas, until the peas are very tender. Remove about 3 tablespoons of the peas, using a slotted spoon, and put to one side for the garnish.

3 Pour the soup into a food processor or blender, add the milk and purée until smooth. Then return the soup to the pan and reheat gently. Season to taste, adding a pinch of sugar, if liked.

4 Pour the soup into individual bowls. Swirl a little cream into each, then garnish with mint and the reserved peas.

Carrot and Coriander Soup

Use a good homemade stock for this soup – it adds a far greater depth of flavor than stock made from cubes.

INGREDIENTS

Serves 4

4 tablespoons butter

3 leeks, sliced

1 pound carrots, sliced

1 tablespoon ground coriander

5 cups homemade/canned chicken stock

$^2/_3$ cup plain yogurt, preferably sheep's milk

salt and black pepper

2–3 tablespoons chopped cilantro, to garnish

1 Melt the butter in a large pan. Add the leeks and carrots and stir well to coat with the butter. Cover and cook for about 10 minutes, until the vegetables are beginning to soften but not color.

2 Stir in the ground coriander and cook for about 1 minute. Pour in the stock and season to taste. Bring to a boil, cover, and simmer for about 20 minutes, until the leeks and carrots are tender.

3 Let cool slightly, then purée the soup in a blender until smooth. Return the soup to the pan and add 2 tablespoons of the yogurt, then taste the soup and adjust the seasoning. Reheat gently but do not boil.

4 Ladle the soup into bowls and add a spoonful of yogurt to the center of each. Sprinkle on the cilantro and serve immediately.

Leek, Potato and Arugula Soup

Arugula, with its distinctive, peppery taste, is wonderful in this deliciously filling soup. Serve it hot with Italian bread croutons.

INGREDIENTS

Serves 4–6

4 tablespoons butter

1 onion, chopped

3 leeks, chopped

2 potatoes, diced

$3^3/4$ cups light homemade or canned
   chicken stock

2 large handfuls arugula,
   coarsely chopped

$2/3$ cup heavy cream

salt and black pepper

garlic-flavored croutons, to serve

1 Melt the butter in a large heavy-bottomed pan, add the onion, leeks and potatoes and stir until the vegetables are coated.

2 Cover and let the vegetables sweat for about 15 minutes. Pour in the stock, cover once again, then simmer the vegetables for 20 minutes, until tender.

3 Press the soup through a sieve or food mill and return to the rinsed-out pan. (When puréeing the soup, don't use a blender or food processor, as these will give the soup a gluey texture.) Add the chopped arugula and cook gently for 5 minutes.

4 Stir in the cream, then season to taste and reheat gently. Ladle the soup into warm soup bowls and serve with the garlic-flavored croutons.

Split Pea and Zucchini Soup

Rich and satisfying, this tasty and nutritious soup will warm you up on a chilly winter's day.

INGREDIENTS

Serves 4

1 cup yellow split peas
1 medium onion, finely chopped
1 teaspoon sunflower oil
2 medium zucchini, finely diced
4 cups homemade/canned chicken stock
$^1/_2$ teaspoon ground turmeric
salt and black pepper

3 Reserve a handful of zucchini and add the rest to the pan. Cook, stirring, for 2–3 minutes. Add the stock and turmeric and bring to a boil. Reduce the heat, cover and simmer for 30–40 minutes, until the peas are tender.

4 When the soup is almost ready, bring a saucepan of water to a boil, add the reserved diced zucchini and cook for 1 minute, then drain and add to the soup. Adjust the seasoning to taste.

1 Place the split peas in a bowl, cover with cold water and let soak for several hours or overnight. Drain, rinse in cold water and drain again.

2 Cook the onion in the oil in a covered pan, shaking occasionally, until soft.

COOK'S TIP

For a quicker alternative, use split red lentils for this soup – they need no presoaking and cook very quickly. Adjust the amount of stock, if necessary.

Red Bell Pepper Soup with Lime

The beautiful rich red color of this soup makes it a very attractive first course or light lunch. For a special dinner, toast some tiny croutons and serve sprinkled on the soup.

INGREDIENTS

Serves 4–6

4 red bell peppers, seeded and chopped

1 large onion, chopped

1 teaspoon olive oil

1 garlic clove, crushed

1 small red chili, sliced

3 tablespoons tomato paste

3¾ cups homemade or canned
   chicken stock

finely grated rind and juice of 1 lime

salt and black pepper

shreds of lime rind, to garnish

1 Cook the chopped peppers and onion gently in the oil in a covered saucepan for about 5 minutes or until softened, shaking the pan occasionally.

2 Stir in the garlic, then add the chili with the tomato paste. Stir in half the stock, then bring to a boil. Cover the pan and simmer for 10 minutes.

3 Cool slightly, then purée in a food processor or blender. Return to the pan, then add the remaining stock, the lime rind and juice, and seasoning.

4 Bring the soup back to a boil, then serve at once with a few strips of lime rind sprinkled into each bowl.

Jerusalem Artichoke Soup

Topped with saffron cream, this soup is wonderful on a wintry day.

INGREDIENTS

Serves 4

4 tablespoons butter

1 onion, chopped

1 pound Jerusalem artichokes,
    peeled and cut into chunks

$3^3/4$ cups homemade or canned
    chicken stock

$2/3$ cup milk

$2/3$ cup heavy cream

good pinch of saffron powder

salt and black pepper

chopped fresh chives, to garnish

1 Melt the butter in a large heavy-bottomed pan and cook the chopped onion for about 5–8 minutes, until soft but not browned, stirring occasionally.

2 Add the artichokes to the pan and stir until coated in the butter. Cover and cook gently for 10–15 minutes; do not allow the artichokes to brown. Pour in the stock and milk, then cover and simmer for 15 minutes. Cool slightly, then process in a blender or food processor until smooth.

3 Strain the soup back into the pan. Add half the cream, season to taste and reheat gently. Lightly whip the remaining cream with the saffron powder. Ladle the soup into warmed soup bowls and put a spoonful of saffron cream in the center of each. Sprinkle with chopped chives and serve at once.

Broccoli and Stilton Soup

A really easy, but rich, soup – choose something simple to follow, such as plainly roasted or broiled meat, poultry or fish.

INGREDIENTS

Serves 4

12 ounces broccoli

2 tablespoons butter

1 onion, chopped

1 leek, white part only, chopped

1 small potato, cut into chunks

$2^1/2$ cups homemade or canned
    hot chicken stock

$1^1/4$ cups milk

3 tablespoons heavy cream

4 ounces Stilton cheese, no rind, crumbled

salt and black pepper

1 Break the broccoli into florets, discarding any tough stems. Set aside two small, well-shaped florets to use for the garnish

2 Melt the butter in a large pan and cook the onion and leek until soft but not colored. Add the broccoli and potato, then pour in the stock. Cover and simmer for 15–20 minutes, until tender.

3 Cool slightly, then purée the soup in a blender or food processor. Strain through a sieve back into the pan.

4 Add the milk, cream and seasoning to the pan and reheat gently. At the last minute add the cheese, stirring until it just melts. Do not boil.

5 Meanwhile, blanch the reserved broccoli florets and cut them vertically into thin slices. Ladle the soup into warm bowls and garnish with the broccoli and freshly ground black pepper.

Beet and Apricot Swirl

This soup is most attractive if you swirl together the two colored mixtures, but if you prefer, they can be mixed together to save on time and clean-up.

Serves 4

4 large cooked beets, coarsely
 chopped

1 small onion, coarsely chopped

2¹/₂ cups homemade or canned
 chicken stock

1 cup dried apricots

1 cup orange juice

salt and black pepper

1 Place the beets and half the onion in a pan with the stock. Bring to a boil, then reduce the heat, cover, and simmer for about 10 minutes. Purée in a food processor or blender.

2 Place the rest of the onion in a saucepan with the apricots and orange juice, cover, and simmer gently for about 15 minutes, until tender. Process to a purée in a food processor or blender.

3 Return the two mixtures to the saucepans and reheat. Season to taste with salt and pepper, then swirl them together in individual soup bowls for a marbled effect.

COOK'S TIP

The apricot mixture should be the same consistency as the beet mixture – if it is too thick, then add a little more orange juice.

Spicy Corn Soup

If you are using frozen shrimp, then defrost them before adding them to the soup.

INGREDIENTS

Serves 4

^{1}/$_2$ teaspoon sesame or sunflower oil

2 scallions, thinly sliced

1 garlic clove, crushed

2^1/$_2$ cups homemade or canned
    chicken stock

15-ounce can cream-style corn

1^1/$_4$ cups cooked, peeled shrimp

1 teaspoon green chili paste or
    chili sauce (optional)

salt and black pepper

cilantro leaves, to garnish

1 Heat the oil in a large heavy-bottomed saucepan and sauté the scallions and garlic over medium heat for 1 minute, until softened, but not browned.

COOK'S TIP

If cream-style corn is not available, use ordinary canned corn, puréed in a food processor for just a few seconds, until creamy yet with some texture left.

2 Stir in the chicken stock, cream-style corn, shrimp and chili paste or sauce, if using.

3 Bring the soup to a boil, stirring occasionally. Season to taste, then serve at once, sprinkled with cilantro leaves.

Chicken Goujons

Serve as a first course for eight people or as a filling main course for four. Delicious served with baby new potatoes and a green salad.

INGREDIENTS

Serves 8

4 boned and skinned chicken breasts

3 cups fresh breadcrumbs

1 teaspoon ground coriander

2 teaspoons ground paprika

$1/2$ teaspoon ground cumin

3 tablespoons all-purpose flour

2 eggs, beaten

oil, for deep-frying

salt and black pepper

lemon slices, to garnish

sprigs of cilantro, to garnish

For the dip

$1^{1}/4$ cups strained plain yogurt

2 tablespoons lemon juice

4 tablespoons chopped cilantro

4 tablespoons chopped fresh parsley

1 Divide each chicken breast into two natural fillets. Place them between two sheets of plastic wrap and using a rolling pin, flatten each one to a thickness of $1/2$ inch.

2 Cut the chicken into diagonal 1-in strips.

3 Mix the breadcrumbs with the spices and seasoning. Toss the chicken fillet pieces (goujons) in the flour, keeping them separate.

4 Dip the goujons into the beaten egg and then coat with the breadcrumb mixture.

5 Thoroughly combine all the ingredients for the dip and season to taste. Cover and chill until needed.

6 Heat the oil in a heavy-bottomed pan. It is ready for deep-frying when a piece of bread tossed into the oil sizzles on the surface. Fry the goujons in batches until golden and crisp. Drain on paper towels and keep warm in the oven until all the chicken has been fried. Garnish with lemon slices and sprigs of cilantro and serve with the yogurt dip.

Corn-fed Chicken Salad

A light first course for eight or a substantial main course for four.

Serves 8

4 pounds corn-fed or free range chicken

1¼ cups white wine and water, mixed

¼-inch slices French bread

1 garlic clove, peeled

8 ounces green beans, trimmed and cut in
    2-inch lengths

4 ounces fresh young spinach leaves,
    washed and torn into small pieces

2 celery stalks, thinly sliced

2 sun-dried tomatoes, chopped

2 scallions, thinly sliced

fresh chives and parsley, to garnish

For the vinaigrette

2 tablespoons red wine vinegar

6 tablespoons olive oil

1 tablespoon whole-grain mustard

1 tablespoon honey

2 tablespoons chopped mixed fresh herbs

2 teaspoons finely chopped capers

salt and black pepper

2 Put all the ingredients for the vinaigrette into a screw-top jar and shake vigorously. Adjust the seasoning to taste.

3 Toast the French bread until golden brown. Rub with garlic.

4 Cook the green beans in boiling water until just tender. Drain and rinse under cold water.

5 Arrange the spinach on serving plates with the sliced celery, green beans, sun-dried tomatoes, chicken and scallions. Spoon on the dressing, arrange the toasted croutes and garnish with fresh chives and parsley.

1 Preheat the oven to 375°F. Put the chicken, wine and water into a casserole. Roast for 1½ hours, until tender. Let cool in the liquid. Remove the skin and bones and cut the flesh into small pieces.

Chicken Liver Pâté

A deliciously smooth pâté which is ideal to spread on hot toast.

INGREDIENTS

Serves 6 or more

4 tablespoons butter

1 onion, finely chopped

12 ounces chicken livers, trimmed of all dark or greenish parts

4 tablespoons medium sherry

1 ounce cream cheese

1–2 tablespoons lemon juice

2 hard-boiled eggs, chopped

salt and pepper

1/4 cup clarified butter

1 Melt the butter in a frying pan. Add the onion and livers and cook until the onion is soft and the livers are lightly browned and no longer pink in the center.

2 Add the sherry and boil until reduced by half. Cool slightly.

COOK'S TIP

∽

Add brandy instead of sherry for a special occasion dinner party.

3 Turn the mixture into a food processor or blender and add the cream cheese and 1 tablespoon lemon juice. Blend until smooth.

4 Add the hard-boiled eggs and blend briefly. Season with salt and pepper. Taste and add more lemon juice, if desired.

5 Pack the liver pâté into a mold or into individual ramekins. Smooth the surface.

6 Spoon a layer of clarified butter over the surface of the pâté. Chill until firm. Serve at room temperature, with hot toast or crackers.

Chicken and Avocado Mayonnaise

You need really firm scoops or forks to eat this appetizer, so don't be tempted to try to pass it around as a finger food.

INGREDIENTS

Serves 4

2 tablespoons mayonnaise

1 tablespoon ricotta or farmer's cheese

2 garlic cloves, crushed

1 cup chopped cooked chicken

1 large ripe, but firm, avocado, peeled and pitted

2 tablespoons lemon juice

salt and black pepper

corn chips or tortilla chips, to serve

1 Mix together the mayonnaise, ricotta, garlic, and seasoning to taste, in a small bowl. Stir in the chopped chicken.

COOK'S TIP

This mixture also makes a great, chunky filling for sandwiches, rolls or pita bread. Or, serve as a main course salad, heaped onto a base of mixed salad leaves.

2 Chop the avocado and toss immediately in lemon juice.

3 Mix the avocado gently into the chicken mixture. Check the seasoning and chill until needed.

4 Serve in small serving dishes with the corn or tortilla chips as scoops, if desired.

Nutty Chicken Balls

Serve these as a first course with the lemon sauce, or make them into smaller balls and serve on toothpicks as canapés.

1 tablespoon lemon juice
1 tablespoon chopped fresh parsley
1 tablespoon chopped fresh chives

INGREDIENTS

Serves 4

12 ounces chicken
$^1/_2$ cup pistachios, finely
    chopped
1 tablespoon lemon juice
2 eggs, beaten
all-purpose flour, for shaping
$1^1/_4$ cups blanched chopped
    almonds
$^3/_4$ cup dried breadcrumbs
salt and black pepper

For the lemon sauce

$^2/_3$ cup homemade or canned
    chicken stock
1 cup cream cheese

1 Skin and grind or chop the chicken finely. Mix with salt and freshly ground black pepper, pistachios, lemon juice and one beaten egg.

2 Shape into sixteen small balls with floured hands (use a spoon as a guide, so that all the balls are roughly the same size). Roll the balls in the remaining beaten egg and coat first with the almonds and then the dried breadcrumbs, pressing on firmly. Chill until ready to cook.

3 Preheat the oven to 375°F. Place the balls on a greased baking sheet and bake for about 15 minutes, or until golden brown and crisp.

4 To make the lemon sauce, gently heat the chicken stock and cream cheese together in a pan, whisking until smooth. Add the lemon juice, herbs and seasoning. Serve with the chicken balls.

Spiced Chicken Livers

Chicken livers can be bought frozen, but make sure that you defrost them thoroughly before using. Serve as a first course or light meal along with a mixed salad and garlic bread.

INGREDIENTS

Serves 4

12 ounces chicken livers

1 cup all-purpose flour

$1/2$ teaspoon ground coriander

$1/2$ teaspoon ground cumin

$1/2$ teaspoon ground cardamom
  seeds

$1/4$ teaspoon ground paprika

$1/4$ teaspoon ground nutmeg

6 tablespoons olive oil

salt and black pepper

1 Dry the chicken livers on paper towels, removing any unwanted pieces. Cut the large livers in half and leave the smaller ones whole.

2 Mix the flour with all the spices and the seasoning.

3 Coat a few of the livers with spiced flour, separating each piece. Heat the oil in a large frying pan and fry the livers in small batches. (This helps to keep the oil temperature high and prevents the flour from becoming soggy.)

4 Fry quickly, stirring frequently, until crisp. Keep warm, and repeat with the remaining livers. Serve immediately with warm garlic bread and salad.

Mediterranean Tomato Soup

Children will love this soup – especially if you use fancy pasta shapes such as alphabet letters or animals.

INGREDIENTS

Serves 4

1^1/$_2$ pounds ripe plum tomatoes

1 medium onion, quartered

1 celery stalk

1 garlic clove

1 tablespoon olive oil

2 cups homemade or canned
   chicken stock

1 tablespoon tomato paste

^{1}/$_2$ cup small pasta shapes

salt and black pepper

cilantro or parsley, to garnish

1 Put the tomatoes, onion, celery and garlic in a pan with the oil. Cover and cook over low heat for 40–45 minutes, shaking the pan occasionally, until very soft.

2 Spoon the vegetables into a food processor or blender and process until smooth. Press through a sieve back into the pan.

3 Stir in the stock and tomato paste and bring to a boil. Add the pasta and simmer gently for about 8 minutes, or until the pasta is tender. Add salt and pepper to taste, then sprinkle with cilantro or parsley and serve hot.

Mushroom, Celery and Garlic Soup

Worcestershire sauce makes this mushroom soup extra tasty.

INGREDIENTS

Serves 4

4^1/$_2$ cups chopped mushrooms

4 celery stalks, chopped

3 garlic cloves

3 tablespoons dry sherry or white wine

3 cups homemade or canned
   chicken stock

2 tablespoons Worcestershire sauce

1 teaspoon grated nutmeg

salt and black pepper

celery leaves, to garnish

1 Place the mushrooms, celery and garlic in a pan and stir in the sherry or wine. Cover and cook over low heat for about 30–40 minutes, until tender.

2 Add half the stock and purée in a food processor or blender, until smooth. Return to the pan and add the remaining stock, the Worcestershire sauce and nutmeg,

3 Bring to a boil, season to taste and serve hot, garnished with celery leaves.

Chicken Liver and Marsala Pâté

This is a really quick and simple pâté, yet it has a delicious – and quite sophisticated – flavor. It contains Marsala, a soft and pungent fortified wine from Sicily. If it is unavailable, use brandy or a medium-dry sherry.

INGREDIENTS

Serves 4

12 ounces chicken livers, defrosted if frozen

1 cup butter, softened

2 garlic cloves, crushed

1 tablespoon Marsala

1 teaspoon chopped fresh sage

salt and black pepper

8 sage leaves, to garnish

thin, crisp toast, to serve

1 Pick over the chicken livers, then rinse and dry with paper towels. Melt 2 tablespoons of the butter in a frying pan, and fry the chicken livers with the garlic over medium heat for about 5 minutes, or until they are firm but still pink in the middle.

2 Transfer the livers to a blender or food processor, using a slotted spoon, and add the Marsala and chopped sage.

3 Melt 10 tablespoons of the remaining butter in the frying pan, stirring to loosen any residue, then pour into the blender or processor and blend until smooth. Season well.

4 Spoon the pâté into four individual pots and smooth the surface. Melt the remaining butter in a separate pan and pour over the pâtés. Garnish with sage leaves and chill until set. Serve with triangles of toast.

Chicken Lettuce Parcels

Known as Sang Choy *in Hong Kong, this is a popular assemble-it-yourself treat. The filling – an imaginative blend of textures and flavors – is served with crisp lettuce leaves, which are used as wrappers.*

INGREDIENTS

Serves 6

2 chicken breast fillets, total weight about
    12 ounces
4 dried Chinese mushrooms, soaked for
    30 minutes in warm water to cover
2 tablespoons vegetable oil
2 garlic cloves, crushed
6 drained canned water chestnuts,
    thinly sliced
2 tablespoons light soy sauce
1 teaspoon Sichuan peppercorns, dry-fried
    and crushed
4 scallions, finely chopped
1 teaspoon sesame oil
vegetable oil, for deep-frying
2 ounces cellophane noodles
salt and ground black pepper (optional)
1 crisp lettuce, divided into leaves, and
    4 tablespoons hoisin sauce, to serve

1 Remove the skin from the chicken and set aside. Chop the chicken into thin strips. Drain the mushrooms, discard the stems, and slice the caps finely. Set aside.

2 Heat the oil in a wok or large frying pan. Add the garlic, then add the chicken, and stir-fry until the pieces are cooked through and no longer pink.

3 Add the mushrooms, water chestnuts, soy sauce and peppercorns. Toss for 2–3 minutes, then season, if needed. Stir in half the scallions, then the sesame oil. Remove from the heat. Set aside.

4 Heat the oil to 375°F. Test by dropping a cube of bread into the oil: it should brown in 60 seconds. Cut the chicken skin into strips, deep-fry until crisp and drain. Add the noodles to the oil and deep-fry until crisp. Transfer to a plate lined with kitchen paper.

5 Crush the noodles and put them in a serving dish. Top with the chicken skin, chicken mixture and the remaining scallions. Arrange the lettuce leaves on a large platter.

6 Toss the chicken and noodles to mix. Each diner can take one or two lettuce leaves, spread the inside with hoisin sauce and add a spoonful of filling, turning in the sides of the leaves and rolling them into a parcel. The parcels are eaten held in the hand.

Chicken Cigars

These small crispy rolls can be served warm as canapés with a drink before a meal, or as a first course with a crisp, colorful salad.

INGREDIENTS

Serves 4

10-ounce package of filo pastry, defrosted

3 tablespoons olive oil

fresh parsley, to garnish

For the filling

3 cups ground raw chicken

salt and freshly ground black pepper

1 egg, beaten

$1/2$ teaspoon ground cinnamon

$1/2$ teaspoon ground ginger

2 tablespoons raisins

1 tablespoon olive oil

1 small onion, finely chopped

1 Mix all the filling ingredients, except the oil and onion, in a bowl. Heat the oil in a large frying pan and cook the onion until tender. Let cool. Add the mixed filling ingredients.

2 Preheat the oven to 350°F. Once the filo pastry package has been opened, keep the pastry covered at all times with a damp dish towel. Work fast, as the filo pastry dries out very quickly when exposed to the air. Unroll the pastry and cut it into 10 x 4 inch strips.

3 Take a strip (cover the remainder), brush with a little oil and place a small spoonful of filling about $1/2$ inch from the end.

4 To encase the filling, fold the sides inward to a width of 2 inches and roll into a cigar shape. Place on a greased baking sheet and brush with oil. Repeat to use all the filling. Bake for about 20–25 minutes, until golden brown and crisp. Garnish with fresh parsley and serve.

Chicken Roulades

*These chicken rolls make a light
lunch dish for two, or an appetizer
for four. They can be sliced and
served cold with a salad.*

INGREDIENTS

Makes 4

4 chicken thighs, boned and skinned

4 ounces chopped fresh or frozen spinach

1 tablespoon butter

2 tablespoons pine nuts

pinch of grated nutmeg

7 tablespoons fresh white breadcrumbs

4 strips lean bacon

2 tablespoons olive oil

$^2/_3$ cup white wine
   or chicken stock

2 teaspoons cornstarch

2 tablespoons light cream

1 tablespoon chopped fresh chives

salt and black pepper

1 Preheat the oven to 350°F.
Place the chicken thighs
between plastic wrap and flatten
with a rolling pin.

2 Put the spinach and butter into
a saucepan, heat gently until
the spinach has defrosted, if
frozen, then increase the heat and
cook rapidly, stirring occasionally,
until all the moisture has been
cooked off. Add the pine nuts, seasoning, nutmeg and fresh
breadcrumbs.

3 Divide the filling between the
chicken pieces and roll up
neatly. Wrap a strip of bacon
around each piece and tie securely
with fine string.

4 Heat the oil in a large frying
pan and brown the rolls all
over. Lift out, using a slotted spoon
to drain off the oil, and place in a
shallow ovenproof dish.

5 Pour on the wine or stock,
cover, and bake for 15–20
minutes, or until tender. Transfer
the chicken to a serving plate and
remove the string. Strain the
cooking liquid into a saucepan.

6 Blend the cornstarch with a
little cold water and add to the
juices in the pan, along with the
cream. Bring to a boil, stirring
until thick. Adjust the seasoning
and add the chives. Pour the sauce
around the chicken and serve.

Chicken, Bacon and Walnut Terrine

To seal the terrine in the pan for longer storage, pour on melted fat.

INGREDIENTS

Serves 8–10

2 boneless chicken breasts

1 large garlic clove, crushed

$1/2$ slice bread

1 egg

12 ounces bacon (the fattier the better), ground or finely chopped

8 ounces chicken or turkey livers, finely chopped

$1/4$ cup chopped walnuts, toasted

2 tablespoons sweet sherry or Madeira

$1/2$ teaspoon ground allspice

$1/2$ teaspoon cayenne pepper

pinch each ground nutmeg and cloves

8 long strips lean bacon, rind removed

salt and black pepper

chicory leaves and chives, to garnish

1 Cut the chicken breasts into thin strips and season lightly. Mash the garlic, bread and egg together. Work in the chopped bacon (using your hands is really the best way) and then the finely chopped livers. Stir in the chopped walnuts, sherry or Madeira, spices and seasoning to taste.

2 Preheat the oven to 400°F. Stretch out the bacon and use to line a $1^{1}/_{2}$-pound loaf pan, then pack in half the meat mixture.

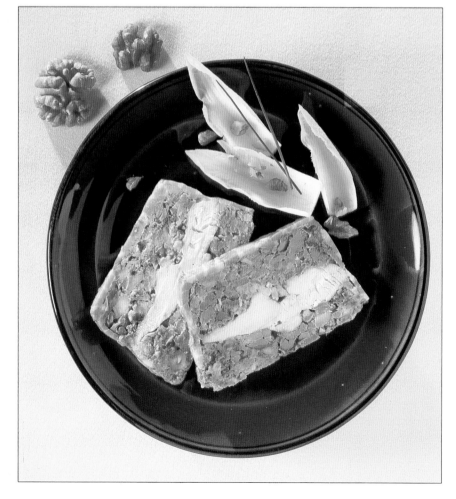

3 Lay the chicken strips on the top and spread the rest of the mixture over. Cover the loaf pan with lightly-greased foil, seal well and press down very firmly.

4 Place the terrine in a roasting pan half-full of hot water and bake for 1–$1^{1}/_{2}$ hours, or until firm to the touch. Remove from the oven, place weights on the top and let cool completely. Drain off any excess fat or liquid while the terrine is warm.

5 When it's really cold, turn out the terrine, cut into thick slices and serve at once, garnished with a few chicory leaves and chives.

Mini Spring Rolls

Use a wok or a large frying pan for this recipe. For a spicier version, sprinkle with a little cayenne pepper.

INGREDIENTS

Makes 20

1 green chili
$^1/_2$ cup vegetable oil
1 small onion, finely chopped
1 clove garlic, crushed
3 ounces cooked chicken breast
1 small carrot, cut into fine matchsticks
1 scallion, finely sliced
1 small red bell pepper, seeded and cut
   into fine matchsticks
1 ounce beansprouts
1 tablespoon sesame oil
4 large sheets filo pastry
egg white, lightly beaten
long chives, to garnish (optional)
3 tablespoons light soy sauce, to serve

1 Carefully remove the seeds from the chili and chop finely, wearing rubber gloves to protect your hands, if necessary.

2 Heat the wok, then add 2 tablespoons of the vegetable oil. When hot, add the onion, garlic and chili. Stir-fry for 1 minute.

3 Slice the chicken thinly, then add to the wok and fry over high heat, stirring and tossing constantly until browned.

4 Add the carrot, scallion and red pepper and stir-fry for 2 minutes. Add the beansprouts, stir in the sesame oil, remove from the heat and let cool.

COOK'S TIP

Always keep filo pastry sheets covered with a damp, clean cloth until needed, to prevent them from drying out.

5 Cut each sheet of filo into 5 short strips. Place a small amount of filling at one end of each strip, then fold in the long sides and roll up the pastry. Seal and glaze the rolls with the egg white, then chill, uncovered, for 15 minutes before frying.

6 Wipe out the wok with paper towels, heat it, and add the remaining vegetable oil. When the oil is hot, fry the rolls in batches, until crisp and golden brown. Drain on paper towels and serve with light soy sauce.

Sesame Seed Chicken Morsels

Stir-fry these crunchy morsels in a wok, then serve them warm with a glass of chilled dry white wine.

INGREDIENTS

Makes 20

6 ounces raw chicken breast

2 cloves garlic, crushed

1-inch piece fresh ginger, peeled and grated

1 medium egg white

1 teaspoon cornstarch

$1/4$ cup shelled pistachios, coarsely chopped

4 tablespoons sesame seeds

2 tablespoons grapeseed oil

salt and black pepper

For the sauce

3 tablespoons hoisin sauce

1 tablespoon sweet chili sauce

To garnish

fresh root ginger, finely shredded

pistachios, coarsely chopped

fresh dill sprigs

1 Place the chicken, garlic, grated ginger, egg white and cornstarch in a food processor or blender and process to a smooth paste.

2 Stir in the pistachios and season with salt and pepper.

3 Roll into 20 balls and coat with sesame seeds. Heat the wok and add the oil. When the oil is hot, stir-fry the chicken in batches, turning regularly until golden. Drain on paper towels.

4 For the sauce, mix together the hoisin and chili sauces in a bowl. Garnish the chicken morsels with shredded ginger, pistachios and dill. Serve hot, with a dish of sauce for dipping.

Spicy Chicken Canapés

These tiny little cocktail sandwiches have a spicy filling and are finished with different toppings. Use square bread so that you can cut out more rounds and have less wastage.

INGREDIENTS

Makes 18

3/4 cup finely chopped cooked
    chicken

2 scallions, finely chopped

2 tablespoons chopped red bell pepper

6 tablespoons Curry Mayonnaise

6 slices white bread

1 tablespoon paprika

1 tablespoon chopped fresh parsley

2 tablespoons chopped salted
    peanuts

2 Spread the mixture over three of the bread slices and sandwich with the remaining bread, pressing well together. Spread the remaining Curry Mayonnaise over the top and cut into 1¹/₂-inch circles using a round cutter.

3 Dip into paprika, chopped parsley or chopped nuts and arrange attractively on a plate.

1 In a bowl, mix the chopped chicken with the chopped scallions, red pepper and half the Curry Mayonnaise.

MIDWEEK
MEALS

Pancake Packages

Making good use of the different types of ground poultry now available, these quick and easy pancakes are filled with a delicious chicken and apple mixture.

INGREDIENTS

Serves 4

For the filling

2 tablespoons oil

4 cups ground chicken

2 tablespoons chopped fresh chives

2 green eating apples, cored and diced

4 tablespoons flour

3/4 cup chicken stock

salt and black pepper

For the pancakes

1 cup all purpose flour

pinch of salt

1 egg, beaten

1 1/4 cups milk

oil for frying

For the sauce

4 tablespoons cranberry sauce

1/4 cup chicken stock

1 tablespoon honey

2 tablespoons cornstarch

1 To make the filling, heat the oil in a large pan and fry the chicken for 5 minutes. Add the chives and apples and then the flour. Stir in the stock and seasoning. Cook for 20 minutes.

2 To make the pancakes, sift the flour into a bowl together with a pinch of salt. Make a well in the center and drop in the egg. Beat it in gradually with the milk to form a smooth batter. Heat the oil in a 6-inch omelet pan. Pour off the oil and add one-quarter of the pancake mixture. Tilt the pan to cover the bottom with the mixture and cook for 2–3 minutes. Turn the pancake over and cook for another 2 minutes. Stack each pancake on top of one another and keep warm.

3 For the sauce, put the cranberry sauce, stock and honey into a pan. Heat gently until melted. Blend the cornstarch with 4 teaspoons cold water, stir it in and bring to a boil. Cook, stirring, until clear.

4 Lay the pancakes on a chopping board, spoon the filling into the center and fold over around the filling. Put on a plate and spoon on the sauce. Serve with a fresh green vegetable.

Chicken Roule

A relatively simple dish to prepare, this recipe uses ground beef as a filling. It is rolled in chicken fillet which is spread with a garlic cheese, which just melts in the mouth.

INGREDIENTS

Serves 4

4 boneless chicken breasts,
    about 4 ounces each
1 cup ground beef
2 tablespoons chopped fresh chives
8 ounces Boursin or garlic
    cream cheese
2 tablespoons honey
salt and black pepper

1 Preheat the oven to 375°F. Place the chicken breasts, side by side, between two pieces of plastic wrap. Beat with a meat mallet until 1/2-inch thick and joined together.

2 Place the ground beef in a large pan. Fry for 3 minutes, add the fresh chives and seasoning. Cool.

3 Place the chicken on a board and spread with the cream cheese.

4 Top with the beef mixture, spreading it over evenly.

5 Roll up the chicken tightly to form a sausage shape.

6 Brush with honey and place in a roasting pan. Cook for 1 hour in the preheated oven. Remove from the pan and slice thinly. Serve with freshly cooked vegetables.

Chicken with Apricot and Pecan Baskets

The potato baskets make a pretty addition to the chicken and could easily have different fillings, if you feel like for a change.

INGREDIENTS

Serves 8

8 chicken breast fillets, about 5 ounces each

6 tablespoons butter

about 2 ounces mushrooms, chopped

1 tablespoon chopped pecan nuts

2/3 cup chopped, cooked ham

1 cup whole wheat breadcrumbs

1 tablespoon chopped parsley, plus some whole leaves to garnish

salt and black pepper

cocktail sticks to secure rolls

For the sauce

1 tablespoon cornstarch

1/2 cup white wine

1/2 cup chicken stock

1/4 cup apricot chutney

For the potato baskets

4 large baking potatoes, about 11 ounces each

6 ounces sausage

8-ounce can apricots in natural juice, drained and quartered

1/4 teaspoon cinnamon

1/2 teaspoon grated orange rind

2 tablespoons maple syrup

2 tablespoons butter

1/4 cup chopped pecan nuts, plus some pecan halves to garnish

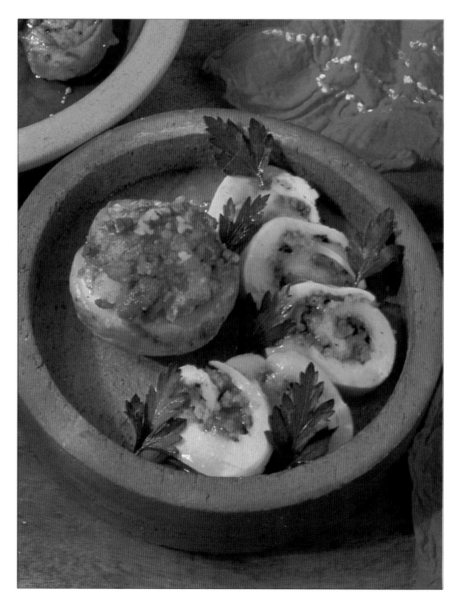

1 Preheat the oven to 400°F and bake the potatoes for 1 1/2 hours, turning once, until soft. Meanwhile, put the chicken between two sheets of greaseproof paper and flatten with a meat pounder. Melt 2 tablespoons of butter in a pan and sauté the mushrooms, pecans and ham. Stir in the breadcrumbs, parsley and seasoning. Divide the mixture between the chicken breasts, roll up and secure each one with a cocktail stick. Chill.

2 Mix the cornstarch with a little of the wine to make a paste. Put the remaining wine and stock in a pan, and add the paste. Cook, stirring, until smooth. Add the remaining butter and the chutney and cook for 5 minutes, stirring constantly.

3 Turn down the oven to 350°F. Place the chicken breasts in a shallow ovenproof dish and pour over the sauce. Cover with foil and bake in the oven for 20–25 minutes until cooked.

4 When the potatoes are cooked, cut them in half and scoop out the inside. Mash the potato and place in a mixing bowl.

5 Fry the sausage and drain off any fat. Add the remaining ingredients and cook for 1 minute. Mix together the sausage and potato and put in the potato shells. Sprinkle the pecan halves over the top, put in the oven with the chicken and bake for 20–25 minutes.

6 Remove the chicken and drain the sauce into a separate dish. Slice the breasts, put on to plates and pour the sauce over the top. Serve with the potato baskets.

Chicken with Yellow Pepper Sauce

*Scallops of chicken filled with garlic
cheese with yellow pepper sauce.*

INGREDIENTS

Serves 4

2 tablespoons olive oil

2 large yellow bell peppers, seeded and
   chopped

1 small onion, chopped

1 tablespoon fresh squeezed orange juice

1¹/₄ cups homemade/canned chicken
   stock

4 chicken breasts

3 ounces Boursin or garlic cream cheese

12 fresh basil leaves

2 tablespoons butter

salt and black pepper

1 To make the yellow pepper
   sauce, heat half the oil in a pan
and gently fry the peppers and
onion until beginning to soften.
Add the orange juice and stock and
cook until very soft.

2 Meanwhile, lay the chicken
   fillets out flat and pound
them lightly.

3 Spread the chicken fillets with
   the Boursin or garlic cream
cheese. Chop half the basil and
sprinkle on top, then roll up the
fillets, tucking in the ends like an
envelope, and secure neatly with
half a toothpick.

4 Heat the remaining oil and the
   butter in a frying pan and fry
the fillets for 7–8 minutes, turning
them frequently, until golden and
cooked through.

5 While the fillets are cooking,
   press the pepper mixture
through a sieve, or blend until
smooth, then strain back into the
pan. Season to taste and warm
through, or serve cold, with the
fillets, garnished with the remaining basil leaves.

COOK'S TIP

Turkey or veal scallops could be
used in place of the chicken,
if you prefer.

Chili Chicken Couscous

Couscous is a convenient alternative to rice and makes a good base for all kinds of ingredients.

INGREDIENTS

Serves 4

2 cups couscous

4 cups boiling water

1 teaspoon olive oil

14 ounces chicken without
    skin and bone, diced

1 yellow bell pepper, seeded and sliced

2 large zucchini, sliced thickly

1 small green chili, thinly sliced,
    or 1 teaspoon chili sauce

1 large tomato, diced

15-ounce can chickpeas, drained

salt and black pepper

cilantro or parsley sprigs to garnish

1 Place the couscous in a large bowl and pour boiling water over it. Cover and let stand for 30 minutes.

2 Heat the oil in a large, non-stick pan and stir-fry the chicken quickly, then reduce the heat.

3 Stir in the pepper, zucchini and chili or sauce and cook for about 10 minutes, until the vegetables are softened.

4 Stir in the tomato and chick-peas, then add the couscous. Adjust the seasoning and stir over medium heat until hot. Serve garnished with sprigs of fresh cilantro or parsley.

Chicken Bean Bake

Sliced eggplant layered with beans and chicken and topped with yogurt.

INGREDIENTS

Serves 4

1 medium eggplant, thinly sliced

1 tablespoon olive oil, for brushing

1 pound boneless chicken breast, diced

1 medium onion, chopped

14-ounce can chopped tomatoes

15-ounce can red kidney beans, drained

1 tablespoon paprika

1 tablespoon chopped fresh thyme,
    or 1 teaspoon dried

1 teaspoon chili sauce

1 1/2 cups strained plain yogurt

1/2 teaspoon nutmeg

salt and black pepper

1 Preheat the oven to 375°F. Arrange the eggplant in a colander and sprinkle with salt.

2 Set the eggplant aside for 30 minutes, then rinse and pat dry. Brush a nonstick pan with oil and fry the eggplant in batches, turning once, until golden.

3 Remove the eggplant, add the chicken and onion to the pan, and cook until lightly browned.

Stir in the tomatoes, beans, paprika, thyme, chili sauce and seasoning. In a bowl, combine the yogurt and nutmeg.

4 Layer the meat and eggplant in an ovenproof dish, finishing with eggplant. Spread the yogurt

evenly over the top and bake for 50–60 minutes, until golden.

Chicken Spirals

These little spirals look impressive, but they're very simple to make, and a good way to jazz up plain chicken.

Serves 4

4 chicken breasts, about 3^1/$_2$ ounces
   each, thinly sliced

4 teaspoons tomato paste

^{1}/$_2$ cup large basil
   leaves

1 garlic clove, crushed

1 tablespoon skim milk

2 tablespoons whole wheat flour

salt and black pepper

puréed tomatoes or fresh tomato sauce
   and pasta, to serve

1 Place the chicken breasts on a
board. If too thick, flatten them
slightly by beating with a rolling
pin or meat market.

2 Spread each chicken fillet with
tomato paste, then top with a
few basil leaves, a little crushed
garlic and seasoning.

3 Roll up firmly around the
filling and secure with a
toothpick. Brush with milk and
sprinkle with flour to coat lightly.

4 Place the spirals on a foil-lined
broiler pan. Cook them under
a medium-hot broiler for 15–20
minutes, turning occasionally,
until thoroughly cooked. Serve
hot, sliced, with a spoonful or two
of puréed tomatoes or sauce and
accompanied with pasta sprinkled
with fresh basil.

COOK'S TIP
~
When flattening the chicken
fillets with a rolling pin, place
them between two sheets of
plastic wrap.

Monday Savory Omelet

*Use up all your leftover odds and
ends in this tasty omelet.*

INGREDIENTS

Serves 4–6

2 tablespoons olive oil

1 large onion, chopped

2 large garlic cloves, crushed

4 ounces rindless bacon, chopped

2 ounces cold cooked chicken, chopped

4 ounces leftover cooked vegetables
   (preferably ones which are not too soft)

1 cup leftover cooked rice or pasta

4 eggs

2 tablespoons chopped, mixed fresh
   herbs, such as parsley, chives, marjoram
   or tarragon, or 2 teaspoons dried

1 teaspoon Worcestershire sauce,
   or more to taste

1 tablespoon grated aged
   Cheddar cheese

salt and black pepper

1 Heat the oil in a large flameproof frying pan and sauté the
onion, garlic and bacon until all
the fat has run out of the bacon.

2 Add the chopped chicken,
vegetables and rice (or pasta).
Beat the eggs, herbs and
Worcestershire sauce together
with seasoning. Pour over the
rice (or pasta) and vegetables, stir
lightly, then leave the mixture
undisturbed to cook gently for
about 5 minutes.

3 When just beginning to set,
sprinkle with the cheese and
place under a preheated broiler
until just firm and golden.

COOK'S TIP

This is surprisingly good cold, so
it's perfect for taking on picnics,
or using for packed lunches.

Chicken Lasagne

Based on the Italian beef lasagne, this is an excellent dish for entertaining guests of all ages. Serve simply with a green salad.

INGREDIENTS

Serves 8

2 tablespoons olive oil

2 pounds ground chicken

1½ cups rindless lean bacon strips, chopped

2 garlic cloves, crushed

1 pound leeks, sliced

1¼ cups carrots, diced

2 tablespoons tomato paste

2 cups homemade/canned chicken stock

12 sheets (no need to pre-cook) green lasagne

For the cheese sauce

4 tablespoons butter

½ cup all-purpose flour

2½ cups milk

1 cup grated aged Cheddar cheese

¼ teaspoon dry English mustard

salt and black pepper

1 Heat the oil in a large flame-proof casserole and brown the ground chicken and bacon briskly, separating the pieces with a wooden spoon. Add the crushed garlic cloves, sliced leeks and diced carrots and cook for about 5 minutes until softened. Add the tomato paste, stock and seasoning. Bring to a boil, cover and simmer for 30 minutes.

2 To make the sauce, melt the butter in a saucepan, add the flour and gradually blend in the milk, stirring until smooth. Bring to a boil, stirring all the time, until thickened and simmer for several minutes. Add half the grated cheese and the mustard, and season to taste.

3 Preheat the oven to 375°F. Layer the chicken mixture, lasagne and half the cheese sauce in a 10-cup ovenproof dish, starting and finishing with a layer of chicken.

4 Pour the remaining half of the cheese sauce over the top to cover, sprinkle on the remaining cheese and bake in the preheated oven for 1 hour, or until bubbling and lightly browned on top.

Crunchy Stuffed Chicken Breasts

These can be prepared ahead of time as long as the stuffing is entirely cold before the chicken is stuffed. It is an ideal dish for entertaining.

INGREDIENTS

Serves 4

4 chicken breasts, boned
2 tablespoons butter
1 garlic clove, crushed
1 tablespoon Dijon mustard

For the stuffing

1 tablespoon butter
1 bunch scallions, sliced
3 tablespoons fresh breadcrumbs
2 tablespoons pine nuts
1 egg yolk
1 tablespoon chopped fresh parsley
salt and black pepper
4 tablespoons grated cheese

For the topping

2 bacon slices, finely chopped
1 cup fresh breadcrumbs
1 tablespoon grated Parmesan cheese
1 tablespoon chopped fresh parsley

1 Preheat the oven to 400°F. To make the stuffing, heat 1 tablespoon of the butter in a frying pan and cook the scallions until soft. Remove from the heat and allow to cool for a few minutes.

2 Add the remaining ingredients and mix thoroughly.

3 To make the topping, fry the chopped bacon until crisp, drain and add to the breadcrumbs, Parmesan cheese and fresh parsley.

4 Carefully cut a deep pocket in each of the chicken breasts, using a sharp knife.

5 Divide the stuffing into fourths and use to fill the pockets. Put in a buttered ovenproof dish.

6 Melt the remaining butter, mix it with the crushed garlic and mustard, and brush liberally over the chicken. Press on the topping and bake uncovered for about 30–40 minutes, or until tender.

Chicken with Honey and Grapefruit

Chicken breast portions cook very quickly and are ideal for suppers "on-the-run" – but don't be tempted to overcook them. You could substitute boneless turkey breasts, or duck breast fillets for the chicken, if you like.

INGREDIENTS

Serves 4

4 chicken breast portions, skinned

3–4 tablespoons honey

1 pink grapefruit, skinned and
    cut into 12 segments

salt and black pepper

noodles and salad leaves, to serve

1 Make three quite deep, diagonal slits in the chicken flesh, using a large sharp knife.

2 Brush the chicken all over with the honey and sprinkle well with seasoning.

3 Put the chicken in a flameproof dish, the uncut side facing up, and place under a medium broiler for 2–3 minutes.

4 Turn the chicken over and place the grapefruit segments in the slits. Brush with more honey and cook for another 5 minutes, or until tender. If necessary, reduce the heat so that the honey glaze does not burn. Serve at once with noodles and salad leaves.

Crispy Chicken with Garlic Rice

Chicken wings cooked until they are really tender have a surprising amount of meat on them, and make a very economical supper for a crowd of kids – provide lots of paper towels, napkins and finger bowls for the greasy fingers.

INGREDIENTS

Serves 4

1 large onion, chopped

2 garlic cloves, crushed

2 tablespoons sunflower oil

1 1/4 cups basmati rice

1 1/2 cups homemade or canned
    hot chicken stock

2 teaspoons finely grated lemon rind

2 tablespoons chopped mixed herbs

8 or 12 chicken wings

1/2 cup all-purpose flour

salt and black pepper

fresh tomato sauce and
    vegetables, to serve

1 Preheat the oven to 400°F. Fry the onion and garlic in the oil in a large flameproof casserole, until golden. Stir in the rice and toss until all the grains are well coated in oil.

2 Stir in the stock, lemon rind and herbs and bring to a boil. Cover and cook in the middle of the oven for 40–50 minutes. Stir once or twice during cooking.

3 Meanwhile, wipe the chicken wings dry. Season the flour and use to coat the chicken portions thoroughly.

4 Put the chicken wings in a small roasting pan and cook in the top of the oven for 30–40 minutes, turning once, until crisp.

5 Serve the rice and chicken wings with a fresh tomato sauce and a selection of vegetables.

Thai Chicken and Vegetable Stir-fry

Make this easy-to-fix dish a little hotter by adding more fresh ginger.

INGREDIENTS

Serves 4

1 piece lemon grass (or the rind of $^1/_2$ lemon)

$^1/_2$ in piece of fresh ginger

1 large garlic clove

2 tablespoons sunflower oil

10 ounces lean chicken, thinly sliced

$^1/_2$ red bell pepper, seeded and sliced

$^1/_2$ green bell pepper, seeded and sliced

4 scallions, chopped

2 medium carrots, cut into matchsticks

4 ounces thin green beans

2 tablespoons oyster sauce

pinch sugar

salt and black pepper

$^1/_4$ cup salted peanuts, lightly crushed, and cilantro leaves, to garnish

cooked rice, to serve

1 Thinly slice the lemon grass or lemon rind. Peel and chop the ginger and garlic. Heat the oil in a frying pan over a high heat. Add the lemon grass or lemon rind, ginger and garlic, and stir-fry for 30 seconds, or until brown.

2 Add the chicken and stir-fry for 2 minutes. Then add the vegetables and stir-fry for 4–5 minutes, until the chicken is cooked and the vegetables are almost cooked.

3 Finally stir in the oyster sauce, sugar and seasoning to taste and stir-fry for another minute to mix well. Serve immediately, sprinkled with the peanuts and cilantro leaves and accompanied with rice.

Chicken with Herbs and Lentils

Chicken baked on lentils and served topped with garlic butter.

INGREDIENTS

Serves 4

4-ounce piece of thick bacon, rind
   removed, chopped
1 large onion, sliced
2 cups well-flavored homemade or canned
   chicken stock
bay leaf
2 sprigs each parsley, marjoram
   and thyme
1 cup green or brown lentils
4 chicken portions
salt and black pepper
2–4 tablespoons garlic butter

COOK'S TIP

For economy's sake buy a
smallish chicken and cut
it in quarters, to give
generous portions.

1 Fry the bacon gently in a large, heavy-bottomed flameproof casserole until all the fat runs out and the bacon begins to brown. Add the onion and fry for about another 2 minutes.

2 Stir in the chicken stock, bay leaf, herb stalks and some of the leafy parts (keep some herb sprigs for garnish), lentils and seasoning. Preheat the oven to 375°F.

3 Fry the chicken portions in a frying pan to brown the skin before placing on top of the lentils. Sprinkle with seasoning and some of the herbs.

4 Cover the casserole and cook in the oven for about 40 minutes. Serve with a knob of garlic butter on each portion and a few of the remaining herb sprigs.

Minty Yogurt Chicken

Chicken marinated with yogurt,
mint, lemon and honey and broiled.

INGREDIENTS

Serves 4

8 chicken thigh portions, skinned

1 tablespoon honey

2 tablespoons lemon (or lime) juice

2 tablespoons plain yogurt

4 tablespoons chopped fresh mint

salt and black pepper

new potatoes and a tomato salad,
  to serve

1 Slash the chicken flesh at
regular intervals with a sharp
knife. Place in a bowl.

2 Mix together the honey, lime
or lemon juice, yogurt,
seasoning and half the mint.

3 Spoon the marinade over the
chicken and let marinate for
30 minutes. Line the broiler pan
with foil and cook the chicken
under a medium-hot broiler until
thoroughly cooked and golden
brown, turning the chicken
occasionally during cooking.

4 Sprinkle with the remaining
mint and serve with the
potatoes and tomato salad.

Oat-crusted Chicken with Sage

Oats make a good coating for savory foods, and here they offer a tasty way to add extra fiber.

INGREDIENTS

Serves 4

3 tablespoons skim milk

2 teaspoons English mustard

$^1/_2$ cup rolled oats

3 tablespoons chopped sage leaves

8 chicken thighs or drumsticks, skinned

$^1/_2$ cup low-fat cream or farmer's cheese

1 teaspoon whole-grain mustard

salt and black pepper

fresh sage leaves, to garnish

COOK'S TIP

If fresh sage is not available, choose another fresh herb, such as thyme or parsley, rather than a dried alternative.

1 Preheat the oven to 400°F. Mix together the milk and English mustard.

2 Mix the oats with 2 tablespoons of the sage and the seasoning on a plate. Brush the chicken with the milk and roll it in the oats.

3 Place the chicken on a baking sheet and bake for about 40 minutes, or until the juices run clear, not pink, when pierced through the thickest part.

4 Meanwhile, combine the low-fat cheese, whole-grain mustard, remaining sage and seasoning, then serve with the chicken. Garnish the chicken with fresh sage and serve hot or cold.

Tagine of Chicken

Based on a traditional Moroccan dish. The chicken and couscous can be cooked the day before and reheated for serving.

INGREDIENTS

Serves 8

8 chicken legs (thighs and drumsticks)

2 tablespoons olive oil

1 medium onion, finely chopped

2 garlic cloves, crushed

1 teaspoon ground turmeric

$^1/_2$ teaspoon ground ginger

$^1/_2$ teaspoon ground cinnamon

2 cups homemade/canned chicken stock

$1^1/_4$ cups pitted green olives

1 lemon, sliced

salt and black pepper

cilantro sprigs, to garnish

For the vegetable couscous

$2^1/_2$ cups homemade or canned chicken stock

1 pound couscous

4 zucchini, thickly sliced

2 carrots, thickly sliced

2 small turnips, peeled and cubed

3 tablespoons olive oil

1 pound can chickpeas, drained

1 tablespoon chopped cilantro

1 Preheat the oven to 350°F. Cut the chicken legs into two through the joint.

2 Heat the oil in a large flameproof casserole and brown the chicken on both sides. Drain, remove to a dish and keep warm.

3 Add the onion and crushed garlic to the flameproof casserole and cook gently until tender. Add the spices and cook for 1 minute. Pour on the stock, bring to a boil, and return the chicken to the pan. Cover and bake for 45 minutes, until tender. Transfer the chicken to a dish, cover and keep warm.

4 Remove any fat from the cooking liquid and boil to reduce by one-third. Meanwhile, blanch the olives and lemon slices in a pan of boiling water for 2 minutes, until the lemon skin is tender. Drain and add to the cooking liquid, adjusting the seasoning to taste.

5 To cook the couscous, bring the stock to a boil in a large pan and sprinkle in the couscous slowly, stirring all the time. Remove from the heat, cover and let stand for 5 minutes.

6 Meanwhile, cook the prepared vegetables, drain, and put them into a large bowl. Add the couscous and oil and season. Stir the grains to fluff them up, add the chickpeas and finally the chopped cilantro. Spoon onto a large serving plate, cover with the chicken, and spoon on the liquid. Garnish with the cilantro.

Chicken with Asparagus

Canned asparagus may be used instead of fresh, but will not require any cooking – simply add at the very end to warm through.

Serves 4

4 large chicken breasts, boned and
   skinned
1 tablespoon ground cilantro
2 tablespoons olive oil
20 slender asparagus spears, cut
   into 3–4-inch lengths
1^1/$_4$ cups homemade or canned
   chicken stock
1 tablespoon cornstarch
1 tablespoon lemon juice
salt and black pepper
1 tablespoon chopped fresh parsley

1 Split the chicken breasts into two natural fillets. Place each between two sheets of plastic wrap and flatten to a ^{1}/$_4$ inch thickness with a rolling pin. Cut into 1-inch diagonal strips. Sprinkle with cilantro and toss to coat.

2 Heat the oil in a large frying pan and fry the chicken very quickly in small batches for 3–4 minutes, until lightly colored. Season each batch with a little salt and freshly ground black pepper. Remove and keep warm while frying the rest of the chicken.

3 Add the asparagus and chicken stock to the pan and bring to a boil. Cook for another 4–5 minutes, or until tender.

4 Mix the cornstarch to a paste with a little cold water and stir into the sauce to thicken. Return the chicken to the pan and add the lemon juice. Reheat and then serve immediately, garnished with fresh parsley.

Chicken, Carrot and Leek Packages

These intriguing packages may sound fussy for everyday, but they take very little time to make and you can freeze them – ready to cook when defrosted.

INGREDIENTS

Serves 4

4 chicken fillets or boneless breasts

2 small leeks, sliced

2 carrots, grated

4 pitted black olives, chopped

1 garlic clove, crushed

1–2 tablespoons olive oil

8 anchovy fillets

salt and black pepper

black olives and herb sprigs, to garnish

1 Preheat the oven to 400°F. Season the chicken well with salt and pepper.

2 Divide the leeks equally among four sheets of greased waxed paper, about 9 inches square. Place a piece of chicken on top of each one.

3 Mix the carrots, olives, garlic and oil together. Season lightly and place on top of the chicken portions. Top each with two of the anchovy fillets, then carefully wrap up each package, making sure the paper folds are underneath and the carrot mixture on top.

4 Bake for 20 minutes and serve hot, in the paper, garnished with black olives and herb sprigs.

Chicken in a Tomato Coat

Chicken roasted with a coating of tomato sauce and fresh tomatoes.

INGREDIENTS

Serves 4–6

whole free-range chicken,
   3–4¹/₂ pounds

1 small onion

pat of butter

5 tablespoons homemade or canned
   tomato sauce

2 tablespoons chopped, mixed fresh
   herbs, such as parsley, tarragon,
   sage, basil and marjoram, or
   2 teaspoons dried

small glass of dry white wine

2–3 small tomatoes, sliced

olive oil

a little cornstarch (optional)

salt and black pepper

1 Preheat the oven to 375°F. Place the chicken in a roasting pan. Place the onion, the pat of butter and some seasoning inside the chicken.

2 Spread most of the tomato sauce over the chicken and sprinkle with half the herbs and some seasoning. Pour the wine into the roasting pan.

3 Cover with foil, then roast for 1¹/₂ hours, basting occasionally. Remove the foil, spread with the remaining sauce and the sliced tomatoes and drizzle with oil. Continue cooking for another 20–30 minutes, or until the chicken is cooked through.

4 Sprinkle the remaining herbs over the chicken, then carve into portions. Thicken the sauce with a little cornstarch if you like.

Chicken Stroganoff

Based on the classic Russian dish, usually made with beef. Serve with rice mixed with chopped celery and scallions.

INGREDIENTS

Serves 4

4 large chicken breasts, boned and
   skinned

3 tablespoons olive oil

1 large onion, thinly sliced

3 cups mushrooms, sliced

1¼ cups sour cream

salt and black pepper

1 tablespoon chopped fresh parsley,
   to garnish

1 Split the chicken breasts into two natural fillets, place between two sheets of plastic wrap and flatten each to a thickness of ¹/₂ inch with a rolling pin.

2 Cut into 1-inch strips diagonally across the fillets.

3 Heat 2 tablespoons of the oil in a frying pan and cook the onion slowly until soft but not colored.

4 Add the mushrooms and cook until golden brown. Remove and keep warm.

5 Increase the heat, add the remaining oil and fry the chicken very quickly, in small batches, for 3–4 minutes, until lightly colored. Remove to a dish and keep warm.

6 Return all the chicken, onions and mushrooms to the pan and season with salt and black pepper. Stir in the sour cream and bring to a boil. Sprinkle with fresh parsley and serve immediately.

Chicken Pancakes

A good way of using up leftover cooked chicken and frozen pancakes.

INGREDIENTS

Serves 4

8 ounces cooked, boned chicken

2 tablespoons butter

1 small onion, finely chopped

$3/4$ cup mushrooms, finely chopped

2 tablespoons all-purpose flour

$2/3$ cup homemade or canned chicken stock or milk

1 tablespoon chopped fresh parsley

8 small or 4 large cooked pancakes

oil, for brushing

2 tablespoons grated cheese

salt and black pepper

1 Remove the skin from the chicken and cut into cubes.

2 Heat the butter in a saucepan and cook the onion gently until tender. Add the mushrooms. Cook, covered, for another 3–4 minutes.

3 Add the flour and then the stock or milk, stirring constantly. Boil to thicken and simmer for 2 minutes. Season with salt and black pepper.

4 Add the chicken cubes and chopped fresh parsley.

5 Divide the filling equally between the pancakes, roll up and arrange in a greased oven-proof dish. Preheat the broiler.

6 Brush the pancakes with a little oil and sprinkle with cheese. Broil until browned. Serve hot.

Lemon Chicken Stir-fry

It is essential to prepare all the ingredients before you begin so they are ready to cook. This dish is cooked in minutes.

INGREDIENTS

Serves 4

4 chicken breasts, boned and skinned

1 tablespoon light soy sauce

5 tablespoons cornstarch

1 bunch scallions

1 lemon

1 garlic clove, crushed

1 tablespoon sugar

2 tablespoons sherry

$^2/_3$ cup homemade or canned
chicken stock

4 tablespoons olive oil

salt and black pepper

1 Split the chicken breasts into two natural fillets. Place each between two sheets of plastic wrap and flatten to a thickness of $^1/_4$ inch with a rolling pin.

2 Cut into 1-inch strips across the grain of the fillets. Put in a bowl with the soy sauce and toss to coat. Sprinkle on 4 tablespoons of the cornstarch and toss.

3 Trim off the roots and cut the scallions diagonally into $^1/_2$-inch pieces. With a vegetable peeler, remove the lemon rind in thin strips and cut into fine shreds, or grate finely. Reserve the lemon juice. Blend the garlic, sugar, sherry, stock, lemon juice and remaining cornstarch into a paste, with water.

4 Heat the oil in a wok or large frying pan and cook the chicken very quickly in small batches for 3–4 minutes, until lightly colored. Remove to a dish and keep warm.

5 Add the scallions and garlic to the pan and cook for 2 minutes.

6 Add the remaining ingredients, with the chicken, and bring to a boil, stirring until thickened. Add more sherry or stock, if necessary, and stir until the chicken is evenly covered with sauce. Reheat for about 2 minutes.

Crispy Spring Chickens

These small birds can be roasted in the oven fairly quickly and are delicious either hot or cold.

INGREDIENTS

Serves 4

2 chickens, 2 pounds each
salt and black pepper

For the honey glaze
2 tablespoons honey
2 tablespoons sherry
1 tablespoon vinegar

1 Preheat the oven to 350°F. Tie the birds into a neat shape and place on a wire rack over the sink. Pour boiling water over them to plump the flesh and pat dry with paper towels.

2 Mix the honey, sherry and vinegar together and brush over the birds. Season well.

3 Put the rack into a roasting pan and roast the birds for 45–55 minutes. Baste well during cooking with the honey glaze until crisp and golden brown.

Chicken Cordon Bleu

A rich dish, popular with cheese lovers. Serve simply with green beans and tiny baked potatoes, cut and filled with cream cheese.

INGREDIENTS

Serves 4

4 chicken breasts, boned and
    skinned

4 slices lean ham

4 tablespoons grated Gruyère or
    Emmental cheese

2 tablespoons olive oil

1$\frac{1}{4}$ cups button mushrooms, sliced

4 tablespoons white wine

salt and black pepper

watercress, to garnish

1 Place the chicken between two pieces of plastic wrap and flatten to a thickness of $\frac{1}{4}$ inch with a rolling pin. Place the chicken breasts, outer side down, on the board and lay a slice of ham on each. Divide the cheese between the chicken breasts and season with a little salt and freshly ground pepper.

2 Fold the chicken breasts in half and secure with wooden toothpicks, making a large "stitch" to hold the pieces together.

3 Heat the oil in a large frying pan and brown the chicken breasts on all sides. Remove to a dish and keep warm.

4 Add the mushrooms to the pan and cook for several minutes to brown lightly. Replace the chicken and pour in the wine, cover, and cook gently for 15–20 minutes, until tender. Remove the toothpicks and arrange on a serving dish with a bunch of watercress.

Chicken in Herb Crusts

The chicken breasts can be brushed with melted butter instead of mustard before being coated in the breadcrumb mixture. Serve with new potatoes and salad.

INGREDIENTS

Serves 4

4 chicken breasts, boned and skinned

1 tablespoon Dijon mustard

1 cup fresh breadcrumbs

2 tablespoons chopped fresh parsley

1 tablespoon mixed dried herbs

2 tablespoons butter, melted

salt and black pepper

2 Mix the breadcrumbs and herbs together thoroughly.

3 Press onto the chicken to coat. Spoon on the melted butter. Bake uncovered for 20 minutes, or until tender and crisp.

1 Preheat the oven to 350°F. Lay the chicken breasts in a greased ovenproof dish and spread with the mustard. Season with salt and freshly ground black pepper.

Tandoori Chicken Kebabs

This dish originated on the plains of the Punjab at the foot of the Himalayas. There, food is traditionally cooked in clay ovens known as tandoors – hence the name.

Serves 4

4 chicken breasts, about 6 ounces each, boned and skinned

1 tablespoon lemon juice

3 tablespoons tandoori paste, available at Indian stores and some supermarkets

3 tablespoons plain yogurt

1 garlic clove, crushed

2 tablespoons chopped cilantro

1 small onion, cut into wedges and separated into layers

a little oil, for brushing

salt and black pepper

cilantro sprigs, to garnish

pilaf rice and naan bread, to serve

1 Chop the chicken breasts into 1-inch cubes, place in a bowl and add the lemon juice, tandoori paste, yogurt, garlic, cilantro and seasoning. Cover and let marinate in the fridge for at least 2–3 hours.

2 Preheat the broiler. Thread alternate pieces of chicken and onion onto four skewers.

3 Brush the onions with a little oil, lay the kebabs on a broiler rack and cook under high heat for about 10–12 minutes, turning once. Garnish the kebabs with cilantro and serve at once with pilaf rice and naan bread.

Chinese Chicken with Cashew Nuts

A stir-fry of chicken with egg noodles, scallions and cashews.

Serves 4

4 chicken breasts about 6 ounces each, boned, skinned and sliced into strips

3 garlic cloves, crushed

4 tablespoons soy sauce

2 tablespoons cornstarch

1 cup dried egg noodles

3 tablespoons peanut or sunflower oil

1 tablespoon sesame oil

1 cup roasted cashews

6 scallions, cut into 2-inch pieces and halved lengthwise

scallion curls and a little chopped red chili, to garnish

1 Put the chicken, garlic, soy sauce and cornstarch in a bowl and mix well. Cover and chill for about 30 minutes.

2 Bring a pan of water to a boil and add the noodles. Turn off the heat and let stand for 5 minutes. Drain well and reserve.

3 Heat the oils in a large frying pan and add the chicken and marinade. Stir-fry for about 3–4 minutes, or until golden brown.

4 Add the cashews and scallions to the pan and stir-fry for 2–3 minutes.

5 Add the drained noodles and stir-fry for another 2 minutes. Serve immediately, garnished with the scallion curls and chopped red chili.

Broiled Rock Cornish Hens with Herbs

Allow one bird per person. Serve with boiled new potatoes and salad.

Serves 4

4 Rock Cornish hens

4 tablespoons butter, melted

1 tablespoon lemon juice

1 tablespoon chopped mixed fresh herbs, such as rosemary and parsley, plus extra to garnish

salt and black pepper

lemon slices, to garnish

1 Remove any trussing strings and, using a pair of kitchen scissors, cut down on either side of the backbone and remove it. Lay the birds flat and flatten with the help of a rolling pin or mallet.

2 Thread the legs and wings onto skewers to keep the hens flat while they are cooking.

3 Brush both sides with melted butter and season with salt and pepper to taste. Sprinkle with lemon juice and herbs.

4 Preheat the broiler to medium heat and cook skin-side first for 6 minutes, until golden brown. Turn over, brush with butter and broil for another 6–8 minutes, or until cooked. Garnish with more chopped herbs and lemon slices.

Chicken Véronique

*True broiling chickens weigh about
2 pounds. If you can't find them, get
the smallest fryers you can.*

INGREDIENTS

Serves 4

2 broiling chickens, about 2 pounds each

2 fresh tarragon or thyme sprigs

2 tablespoons butter

4 tablespoons white wine

grated rind and juice of $^1/_2$ lemon

1 tablespoon olive oil

1 tablespoon all-purpose flour

$^2/_3$ cup homemade/canned chicken stock

1 cup seedless green grapes,
   cut in half if large

salt and black pepper

chopped fresh parsley, to garnish

1 Preheat the oven to 350°F.
Put the herbs inside the cavity
of each chicken and tie into a
neat shape.

2 Heat the butter in a casserole,
brown the chickens lightly all
over and pour on the wine. Season,
cover, and cook in the oven for
20–30 minutes, or until tender.

3 Remove the chickens from the
casserole and cut in half with a
pair of kitchen scissors, removing
the backbones and small rib cage
bones. Arrange in a shallow ovenproof dish (that will slide under
the broiler). Sprinkle with lemon
juice and brush with oil. Broil until
lightly browned. Keep warm.

4 Mix the flour into the butter
and wine in the casserole,
and blend in the stock. Bring to a
boil, season to taste, add the lemon
rind and grapes, then simmer for
2–3 minutes. Spoon the sauce on
the chickens, garnish with fresh
parsley and serve immediately.

Chicken with Orange and Mustard Sauce

The beauty of this recipe is its simplicity; the chicken continues to cook in its own juices while you prepare the sauce.

INGREDIENTS

Serves 4

4 chicken breasts, boned and skinned

1 teaspoon sunflower oil

salt and black pepper

new potatoes and sliced zucchini
   tossed in parsley, to serve

Orange and mustard sauce

2 large oranges

2 teaspoons cornstarch

²/₃ cup plain yogurt

1 teaspoon Dijon mustard

1 Peel the oranges, using a sharp knife, removing all the white pith. Remove the segments by cutting between the membranes, holding the fruit over a small bowl to catch any juice. Set aside with the juice until needed.

2 Season the chicken with salt and freshly ground black pepper. Heat the oil in a nonstick frying pan and cook the chicken breasts for 5 minutes on each side. Take out of the frying pan and wrap in foil; the meat will continue to cook for awhile.

3 To make the sauce, blend together the cornstarch with the juice from the oranges. Add the yogurt and mustard. Put into the frying pan and slowly bring to a boil. Simmer for 1 minute.

4 Add the orange segments to the sauce and heat gently. Unwrap the chicken and add any excess juices to the sauce. Slice on the diagonal and serve with the sauce, new potatoes and sliced zucchini tossed in parsley.

Chicken and Chorizo

The perfect way to use up leftover cold meat – this spicy dish is a fast, fortifying meal for a hungry family.

Serves 4

3 tablespoons vegetable oil

1 medium onion, chopped

1 celery stalk, chopped

$^1/_2$ red bell pepper, chopped

2 cups long-grain rice

4 cups homemade/canned chicken stock

1 tablespoon tomato paste

3–4 shakes of Tabasco sauce

8 ounces cold roast chicken or pork, thickly sliced

4 ounces cooked sausage, such as chorizo or Polish, sliced

3 ounces frozen peas

3 Stir in the cold meat, sausage and peas and simmer for another 5 minutes. Switch off the heat, cover and let stand for 5 minutes more before serving.

VARIATIONS

You could also add cooked ham, smoked cod or haddock and fresh shellfish to this dish.

1 Heat the oil in a heavy-bottomed saucepan and add the onion, celery and pepper. Cook to soften, without coloring.

2 Add the rice, chicken stock, tomato paste and Tabasco sauce. Simmer uncovered for about 10 minutes.

Chicken Cutlets with Olives

This quick and tasty dish makes a good light main course.

INGREDIENTS

Serves 4

6 tablespoons olive oil

1 clove garlic, peeled and lightly
  crushed

1 dried chili, lightly crushed

1$^1/_4$ pounds boneless chicken breast,
  cut into $^1/_4$-inch slices

$^1/_2$ cup dry white wine

4 tomatoes, peeled and seeded,
  cut into thin strips

about 24 black olives

6–8 leaves fresh basil, torn into pieces

salt and black pepper

1 Heat 4 tablespoons of the olive oil in a large frying pan. Add the garlic and crushed dried chili, and cook over low heat until the garlic is golden.

2 Raise the heat to medium and add remaining oil. Place the chicken slices in the pan, and brown them lightly on both sides for about 2 minutes. Season with salt and pepper. Remove the chicken to a heated dish.

3 Discard the garlic and chili. Add the wine, tomato strips and olives. Cook over medium heat for 3–4 minutes, scraping up any residue from the bottom of the pan.

4 Return the chicken to the pan. Sprinkle with the torn basil. Heat through for 30 seconds, and serve at once.

Mediterranean Chicken Skewers

These skewers are easy to assemble, and can be cooked under the broiler or on a charcoal grill.

Serves 4

6 tablespoons olive oil

3 tablespoons fresh lemon juice

1 clove garlic, finely chopped

2 tablespoons chopped fresh basil

2 medium zucchini

1 long thin eggplant

11 ounces boneless chicken, cut into
   2-inch cubes

12–16 pickled onions

1 bell pepper, red or yellow, cut into
   2-inch squares

salt and black pepper

1 In a small bowl, mix the oil with the lemon juice, garlic and basil. Season with salt and pepper.

2 Slice the zucchini and eggplant lengthwise into strips ¼-inch thick. Cut them horizontally about two-thirds of the way along their length. Discard the shorter length. Wrap half the chicken pieces with the zucchini slices, and the other half with the eggplant slices.

3 Prepare the skewers by alternating the chicken, onions and pepper pieces. Lay the prepared skewers on a platter, and sprinkle with the flavored oil. Let marinate for at least 30 minutes. Preheat the broiler, or prepare a charcoal grill.

4 Broil or grill for about 10 minutes, or until the vegetables are tender, turning the skewers occasionally. Serve hot.

Rock Cornish Hens with Dirty Rice

This rice is called dirty not because of the bits in it (though the roux and chicken livers do "muss" it up a bit) but because jazz is called "dirty music," and the rice in this recipe is certainly jazzed up.

INGREDIENTS

Serves 4

For the rice

4 tablespoons cooking oil

$^1/_4$ cup all-purpose flour

4 tablespoons butter

1 large onion, chopped

2 celery stalks, chopped

1 green bell pepper, seeded and diced

2 garlic cloves, crushed

7 ounces ground pork

8 ounces chicken livers, trimmed
    and sliced

Tabasco sauce

$1^1/_4$ cups homemade or canned
    chicken stock

4 scallions, shredded

3 tablespoons chopped fresh parsley

1 cup American long-grain
    rice, cooked

salt and black pepper

For the birds

4 Rock Cornish hens

2 bay leaves, halved

2 tablespoons butter

1 lemon

COOK'S TIP

If available, try substituting quails for the Rock Cornish hens, in which case offer two per person and stuff each little bird with 2 teaspoons of dirty rice before roasting for about 20 minutes.

---

1 In a small heavy-bottomed saucepan, make a roux by blending together 2 tablespoons of the oil and the flour. When it is a chestnut brown color, remove the pan from the heat and place it immediately on a cold surface.

2 Heat the remaining 2 tablespoons oil with the butter in a frying pan and stir-fry the onion, celery and green bell pepper for about 5 minutes.

3 Add the garlic and pork and stir-fry for about 5 minutes, breaking up the pork and stirring well to cook it all over.

4 Add the chicken livers and fry for 2–3 minutes until they have changed color all over. Season with salt and black pepper and a dash of Tabasco sauce.

5 Stir the roux into the stir-fried mixture, then gradually add the stock. When it begins to bubble, cover and cook for 30 minutes, stirring occasionally. Uncover and cook for another 15 minutes, stirring frequently.

6 Preheat the oven to 400°F. Mix the shredded scallions and chopped parsley into the meat mixture and stir it all into the cooked rice.

7 Put $^1/_2$ bay leaf and 1 tablespoon rice into each bird. Rub the outside with the butter and season with salt and pepper.

8 Put the birds on a rack in a roasting pan, squeeze the juice from the lemon over them and roast in the oven for 35–40 minutes, basting twice during cooking with the pan juices.

9 Put the remaining rice into a shallow ovenproof dish, cover it and place on a low rack in the oven for the last 15–20 minutes of the birds' cooking time.

10 Serve the birds on a bed of dirty rice with the roasting juices (drained of fat) poured on top.

Chicken Kiev

Cut through the crispy-coated chicken to reveal a creamy filling with just a hint of garlic.

INGREDIENTS

Serves 4

4 large chicken breasts, boned and
    skinned
1 tablespoon lemon juice
$1/2$ cup ricotta cheese
1 garlic clove, crushed
2 tablespoons chopped fresh parsley
$1/4$ teaspoon freshly grated nutmeg
2 tablespoons all-purpose flour
pinch of cayenne pepper
$1/4$ teaspoon salt
2 cups fresh white breadcrumbs
2 egg whites, lightly beaten
creamed potatoes, green beans and
    broiled tomatoes, to serve

1 Preheat the oven to 400°F. Place the chicken breasts between two sheets of plastic wrap and gently beat with a rolling pin until flattened. Sprinkle with the lemon juice.

2 Mix the ricotta cheese with the garlic, 1 tablespoon of the chopped parsley and the nutmeg. Shape into four 2-inch long rolls.

3 Put one portion of the cheese and herb mixture in the center of each chicken breast and fold the meat over, tucking in the edges to enclose the filling completely.

4 Secure the chicken with toothpicks pushed through the center of each. Mix together the flour, cayenne pepper and salt and use to dust the chicken.

5 Mix together the breadcrumbs and remaining parsley. Dip the chicken into the egg whites, then coat with the breadcrumbs. Chill for 30 minutes in the fridge, then dip into the egg white and breadcrumbs for a second time.

6 Put the chicken on a nonstick baking sheet. Bake in the preheated oven for 25 minutes, or until the coating is golden brown and the chicken completely cooked. Remove the toothpicks and serve with creamed potatoes, green beans and broiled tomatoes.

Stuffed Rock Cornish Hens

Port wine-soaked raisins, walnuts and mushrooms make an unusual stuffing for Rock Cornish hens.

Serves 4

1 cup Port wine

$1/3$ cup raisins

1 tablespoon walnut oil

3 ounces mushrooms, minced

1 large celery stalk, minced

1 small onion, chopped

salt and pepper

1 cup fresh breadcrumbs

$1/2$ cup chopped walnuts

1 tablespoon each chopped fresh
   basil and parsley, or 2 tablespoons
   chopped parsley

$1/2$ teaspoon dried thyme

6 tablespoons butter, melted

4 Rock Cornish hens

1 Preheat the oven to 350°F.

2 In a small bowl, combine the Port wine and raisins and let soak for about 20 minutes.

3 Meanwhile, heat the oil in a nonstick pan. Add the mushrooms, celery, onion and $1/4$ teaspoon salt and cook over low heat until softened, about 8–10 minutes. Set aside to cool.

4 Drain the raisins, reserving the Port wine. Combine the raisins, breadcrumbs, walnuts, basil, parsley and thyme in a bowl. Stir in the onion mixture and 4 tablespoons of the melted butter. Add $1/2$ teaspoon salt and pepper to taste.

5 Fill the cavity of each bird with the stuffing. Do not pack down. Tie the legs together, to enclose the stuffing securely.

6 Brush the birds with the remaining butter and place in a baking dish just large enough to hold them comfortably. Pour on the reserved Port wine.

7 Roast, basting occasionally, for about 1 hour. Test by piercing the thigh with a skewer; the juices should run clear. Serve immediately with some of the juices.

Oven "Fried" Chicken

The chicken in this dish is not fried but baked until crisp in the oven.

INGREDIENTS

Serves 4

4 large chicken pieces

$^1/_2$ cup flour

$^1/_2$ teaspoon salt

$^1/_4$ teaspoon pepper

1 egg

2 tablespoons water

2 tablespoons chopped mixed fresh herbs,
such as parsley, basil and thyme

1 cup dry breadcrumbs

$^1/_3$ cup freshly grated
Parmesan cheese

lemon wedges, for serving

1 Preheat the oven to 400°F.

2 Rinse the chicken in cold water. Pat dry with paper towels.

3 Combine the flour, salt and pepper on a plate and stir with a fork to mix. Coat the chicken pieces on all sides with the flour and shake off the excess.

4 Sprinkle a little water onto the chicken pieces, and coat again lightly with the seasoned flour.

5 Beat the egg with the water in a shallow dish. Stir in the herbs. Dip the chicken pieces into the egg mixture, turning them over to coat them thoroughly.

6 Combine the breadcrumbs and grated Parmesan cheese on a plate. Roll the chicken pieces in the crumbs, patting with your fingers to help them adhere.

7 Place the chicken pieces in a greased shallow pan, large enough to hold them in one layer. Bake until thoroughly cooked and golden brown, 20–30 minutes. To check that they are cooked, prick with a fork; the juices that run out should be clear, not pink. Serve hot, with lemon wedges.

Blackened Chicken Breasts

Chicken breasts with a seasoned coating of herbs and spices.

INGREDIENTS

Serves 6

6 medium chicken breasts,
    boned and skinned

6 tablespoons butter or margarine

1 teaspoon garlic paste

4 tablespoons finely grated onion

1 teaspoon cayenne

2 teaspoons sweet paprika

$1^1/_2$ teaspoons salt

$^1/_2$ teaspoon white pepper

1 teaspoon black pepper

$^1/_4$ teaspoon ground cumin

1 teaspoon dried thyme leaves

1 Slice each chicken breast piece in half horizontally. Flatten them down slightly with the heel of your hand.

2 Melt the butter or margarine in a small saucepan together with the garlic paste.

3 Combine all the remaining ingredients in a shallow bowl and stir well. Brush the chicken pieces on both sides with melted butter or margarine, then sprinkle evenly with the seasoned mixture.

4 Heat a large heavy frying pan over high heat until a drop of water sprinkled on the surface sizzles. This will take 5–8 minutes.

5 Drizzle 1 teaspoon of melted butter on each chicken piece. Place them in the pan in an even layer, 2 or 3 at a time. Cook until the underside begins to blacken, about 2–3 minutes. Turn over and cook 2–3 minutes more, or until the other side blackens. Serve hot.

Chicken Tonnato

This low-fat version of the Italian dish "vitello tonnato" is garnished with fine strips of red pepper instead of the traditional anchovy fillets.

INGREDIENTS

Serves 4

1 pound chicken breasts, boned
   and skinned
1 small onion, sliced
1 bay leaf
4 black peppercorns
1^1/$_2$ cup homemade/canned chicken stock
7-ounce can tuna in water, drained
5 tablespoons reduced fat mayonnaise
2 tablespoons lemon juice
2 red bell peppers, thinly sliced
about 25 capers, drained
pinch of salt
mixed salad and tomatoes, to serve

4 Put the tuna, mayonnaise, lemon juice, 3 tablespoons of the reduced stock and salt into a blender or food processor and purée until smooth.

5 Stir in enough of the remaining stock to reduce the sauce to the thickness of heavy cream. Spoon onto the chicken.

6 Arrange the strips of red pepper in a lattice pattern over the chicken. Put a caper in the center of each square. Chill in the fridge for 1 hour and serve with a fresh mixed salad and tomatoes.

1 Put the chicken breasts in a single layer in a large, heavy-bottomed saucepan. Add the onion, bay leaf, peppercorns and stock. Bring to a boil and reduce the heat. Cover and simmer for about 12 minutes, or until tender.

2 Turn off the heat and let the chicken cool in the stock, then remove with a slotted spoon. Slice the breasts thickly and arrange on a serving plate.

3 Boil the stock until it is reduced to about 5 tablespoons. Strain through a fine sieve and cool.

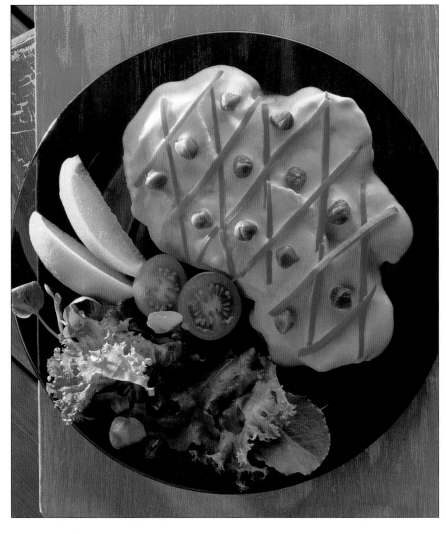

Chicken and Tomato Hot-pot

Versatile ground chicken is perfect for family meals. Here, it's turned into tasty meatballs.

INGREDIENTS

Serves 4

1 slice white bread, crust removed

2 tablespoons milk

1 garlic clove, crushed

$^1/_2$ teaspoon caraway seeds

2 cups ground chicken

1 egg white

$1^1/_2$ cups homemade or canned chicken stock

14-ounce can plum tomatoes

1 tablespoon tomato paste

$^1/_2$ cup long-grain rice

salt and black pepper

1 tablespoon chopped fresh basil

carrot and zucchini ribbons, to serve

4 Put the chicken stock, tomatoes and tomato paste into a large, heavy-bottomed saucepan and bring to a boil.

5 Add the rice, stir, and cook briskly for about 5 minutes. Turn the heat down to a simmer.

6 Meanwhile, shape the chicken mixture into 16 small balls. Carefully drop them into the tomato stock and simmer for another 8–10 minutes, or until the chicken balls and rice are cooked. Garnish with the basil, and serve with carrot and zucchini ribbons.

1 Cut the bread into small cubes and put into a mixing bowl. Sprinkle with the milk and let soak for 5 minutes.

2 Add the garlic clove, caraway seeds, chicken, salt and freshly ground black pepper to the bread. Mix together well.

3 Beat the egg white until stiff, then fold, in two parts, into the chicken mixture. Chill for 10 minutes in the fridge.

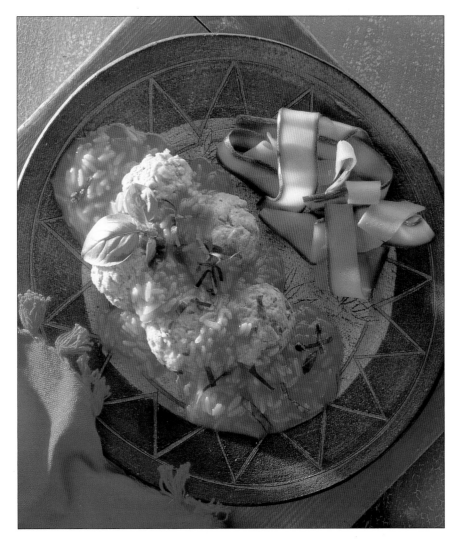

Roast Chicken with Fennel

In Italy this dish is prepared with wild fennel. Cultivated fennel bulb works just as well.

INGREDIENTS

Serves 4–5

1 roasting chicken, about 3^1/$_2$ pounds

1 onion, quartered

^{1}/$_2$ cup olive oil

2 medium fennel bulbs

1 clove garlic, peeled

pinch of grated nutmeg

3–4 thin slices pancetta or bacon

^{1}/$_2$ cup dry white wine

salt and black pepper

1 Preheat the oven to 350°F. Sprinkle the chicken cavity with salt and pepper. Place the onion quarters in the cavity. Rub the chicken with about 3 tablespoons of the olive oil. Place in a roasting pan.

2 Cut the green fronds from the tops of the fennel bulbs. Chop the fronds together with the garlic. Place in a small bowl and mix with the nutmeg and seasoning.

3 Sprinkle the fennel mixture over the chicken, pressing it on the oiled skin. Cover the breast with the slices of pancetta or bacon. Sprinkle with 2 tablespoons of the oil. Place in the oven and roast for 30 minutes.

4 Meanwhile, boil or steam the fennel bulbs until barely tender. Remove from the heat and cut into quarters or sixths lengthwise. After the chicken has been cooking for 30 minutes, remove the pan from the oven. Baste the chicken with any oils in the pan.

5 Arrange the fennel pieces around the chicken. Sprinkle the fennel with the remaining oil. Pour about half the wine on the chicken, and return to the oven.

6 After 30 minutes more, baste the chicken again. Pour on the remaining wine. Cook for 15–20 minutes. To test, prick the thigh with a fork. If the juices run clear, the chicken is cooked. Serve the chicken surrounded by the fennel.

Chicken with Ham and Cheese

This tasty combination comes from Emilia-Romagna, where it is also prepared with veal.

INGREDIENTS

Serves 4

4 small chicken breasts, skinned and boned

flour seasoned with salt and freshly ground black pepper, for dredging

4 tablespoons butter

3–4 leaves fresh sage

4 thin slices prosciutto or ham, cut in half

^{1}/$_2$ cup freshly grated Parmesan cheese

1 Cut each breast in half lengthwise to make two flat fillets of approximately the same thickness. Dredge the chicken in the seasoned flour, and shake off the excess.

2 Preheat the broiler. Heat the butter in a large heavy frying pan and add the sage leaves. Add the chicken, in one layer, and cook over low to medium heat until golden brown on both sides, turning as necessary. This will take about 15 minutes.

3 Remove the chicken from the heat, and arrange on a flameproof serving dish or broiler pan. Place one piece of ham on each chicken fillet and top with the grated Parmesan. Broil for 3–4 minutes, or until the cheese has melted. Serve at once.

Chicken Roll

The roll can be prepared and cooked the day before and will freeze well too. Remove from the fridge about an hour before serving.

INGREDIENTS

Serves 8
1 chicken, about 4¹/₂ pounds

For the stuffing
1 medium onion, finely chopped
4 tablespoons melted butter
2 cups lean ground pork
4 ounces lean bacon, chopped
1 tablespoon chopped fresh parsley
2 teaspoons chopped fresh thyme
2 cups fresh white breadcrumbs
2 tablespoons sherry
1 large egg, beaten
¹/₄ cup shelled pistachios
¹/₄ cup pitted black olives
    (about 12)
salt and black pepper

1 To make the stuffing, cook the chopped onion gently in 2 tablespoons of the butter until soft. Put into a bowl and cool. Add the remaining ingredients, mix thoroughly and season with salt and black pepper.

2 To bone the chicken, use a small, sharp knife to remove the wing tips. Turn the chicken onto its breast and cut a line down the backbone.

3 Cut the meat away from the carcass, scraping the bones clean. Carefully cut through the sinew around the leg and wing joints and scrape down the bones to free them. Remove the carcass, taking care not to cut through the skin along the breastbone.

4 To stuff the chicken, lay it flat, skin side down and flatten as much as possible. Shape the stuffing down the center of the chicken and fold in the sides.

5 Sew the bird neatly together, using a needle and dark thread. Tie with fine string into a roll.

6 Preheat the oven to 350°F. Put the roll, seam side down, on a rack in a roasting pan and brush with the remaining butter. Cook, uncovered, for about 1¹/₄ hours. Baste with the juices during cooking. Let cool. Remove the string and thread. Wrap in foil and chill until needed.

Traditional Roast Chicken

Serve with bacon rolls, small sausages, gravy and stuffing balls.

INGREDIENTS

Serves 4

1 chicken, about 4 pounds

lean bacon strips

2 tablespoons butter

salt and black pepper

For the prune and nut stuffing

2 tablespoons butter

$1/2$ cup chopped pitted prunes

$1/2$ cup chopped walnuts

1 cup fresh breadcrumbs

1 egg, beaten

1 tablespoon chopped fresh parsley

1 tablespoon chopped fresh chives

2 tablespoons sherry or Port

For the gravy

2 tablespoons all-purpose flour

$1^1/4$ cups homemade or canned
    chicken stock

1 Preheat the oven to 375°F. Mix all the stuffing ingredients in a bowl and season well with salt and pepper.

2 Stuff the neck end of the chicken quite loosely, allowing room for the breadcrumbs to swell during cooking. (Any remaining stuffing can be shaped into balls and fried to accompany the roast.)

3 Tuck the neck skin under the bird to secure the stuffing and hold in place with the wing tips, or sew with strong thread or fine string.

4 Place in a roasting pan and cover the breast with the bacon strips. Spread with the remaining butter, cover loosely with foil and roast for about $1^1/2$ hours. Baste with the juices in the roasting pan 3 or 4 times during cooking.

5 Remove any trussing string, transfer to a serving plate, cover with foil and let stand while making the gravy. (This standing time allows the flesh to relax and makes carving easier.)

6 Spoon off the fat from the juices in the pan. Blend in the flour and cook gently until golden brown. Add the stock and bring to a boil, stirring until thickened. Adjust the seasoning and strain into a sauceboat to serve.

Roast Chicken with Celery Root

Chicken with a stuffing of celery root, bacon, onion and herbs.

INGREDIENTS

Serves 4

1 chicken, 3¹/₂ pounds

1 tablespoon butter

For the stuffing

1 pound celery root, chopped

2 tablespoons butter

3 slices bacon, chopped

1 onion, finely chopped

leaves from 1 thyme sprig, chopped

leaves from 1 small tarragon
   sprig, chopped

2 tablespoons chopped
   fresh parsley

1¹/₂ cups fresh brown breadcrumbs

dash of Worcestershire sauce

1 egg, beaten

salt and pepper

1 For the stuffing, cook the celery root in boiling water until tender. Drain well and chop finely.

2 Heat the butter in a saucepan, then gently cook the bacon and onion until the onion is soft. Stir the celery root and herbs into the pan and cook, stirring occasionally, for 2–3 minutes. Meanwhile, preheat the oven to 400°F.

3 Remove the pan from the heat and stir in the fresh bread-crumbs, Worcestershire sauce, seasoning and sufficient egg to bind.

4 Place the stuffing in the neck end of the chicken. Season the bird's skin, then rub with the butter. Roast the chicken, basting occasionally with the juices, for 1¹/₄–1¹/₂ hours, until the juices run clear when the thickest part of the leg is pierced. Rest for 10 minutes in a warm place before carving.

Rock Cornish Hens with Grapes in Vermouth

*A very special dish, ideal to serve
when entertaining.*

INGREDIENTS

Serves 4

4 oven-ready Rock Cornish hens, about
   1 pound each

4 tablespoons butter, softened

2 shallots, chopped

4 tablespoons chopped fresh parsley

8 ounces white grapes, preferably
   muscatel, halved and seeded

$2/3$ cup white vermouth

1 teaspoon cornstarch

4 tablespoons heavy cream

2 tablespoons pine nuts, toasted

salt and black pepper

watercress sprigs, to garnish

1 Preheat the oven to 400°F.
Spread the softened butter all
over the hens and put a hazelnut-
sized piece inside the cavity of
each bird.

2 Mix together the shallots and
parsley and place a quarter of
the mixture inside each hen. Put
the birds side by side in a large
roasting pan and roast for 40–50
minutes, or until the juices run
clear when the thickest part of the
flesh is pierced with a skewer. Put
the birds onto a warm serving
dish, cover and keep warm.

3 Skim off most of the fat from
the roasting pan, then add the
grapes and vermouth. Place the
pan directly over a low flame for a
few minutes to warm and slightly
soften the grapes.

4 Lift the grapes out of the pan
using a slotted spoon and
sprinkle them around the birds.
Keep covered. Stir the cornstarch
into the cream, then add to the pan
juices. Cook gently for a few
minutes, stirring, until the sauce
has thickened. Adjust seasoning.

5 Pour the sauce around the
birds. Sprinkle with the toasted
pine nuts and garnish with
watercress sprigs.

Stir-fried Chicken with Snow Peas

Juicy chicken stir-fried with snow peas, cashews and water chestnuts.

Serves 4

2 tablespoons sesame oil

6 tablespoons lemon juice

1 garlic clove, crushed

$1/2$-inch piece fresh ginger,
    peeled and grated

1 teaspoon honey

1 pound chicken breast fillets,
    cut into strips

4 ounces snow peas, trimmed

2 tablespoons peanut oil

$1/2$ cup cashews

6 scallions, cut into strips

1 can (8-ounces) water chestnuts,
    drained and thinly sliced

salt

saffron rice, to serve

1 Mix together the sesame oil, lemon juice, garlic, ginger and honey in a shallow non-metallic dish. Add the chicken and mix well. Cover and let marinate for at least 3–4 hours.

2 Blanch the snow peas in boiling salted water for 1 minute. Drain and refresh under cold running water.

3 Drain the chicken strips and reserve the marinade. Heat the peanut oil in a wok or large frying pan, add the cashews and stir-fry for about 1–2 minutes until golden brown. Remove the cashews from the wok or frying pan, using a slotted spoon, and set aside.

4 Add the chicken and stir-fry for 3–4 minutes, until golden brown. Add the scallions, snow peas, water chestnuts and the reserved marinade. Cook for a few minutes, until the chicken is tender and the sauce is bubbling and hot. Stir in the cashews and serve with saffron rice.

Stuffed Chicken Breasts with Cream Sauce

Chicken breasts filled with a leek and lime-flavored stuffing and served in a cream sauce.

INGREDIENTS

Serves 4

4 large chicken breasts,
    boned and skinned

4 tablespoons butter

3 large leeks, white and pale green
    parts only, thinly sliced

1 teaspoon grated lime zest

1 cup chicken stock, homemade or
    canned, or half stock and half
    dry white wine

$^1/_2$ cup whipping or
    heavy cream

1 tablespoon lime juice

salt and pepper

1 Cut horizontally into the thickest part of each breast to make a deep, wide pocket. Take care not to cut all the way through. Set the chicken breasts aside.

2 Melt half the butter in a large heavy frying pan over low heat. Add the leeks and lime zest and cook, stirring occasionally, for 15–20 minutes, or until the leeks are very soft but not colored.

3 Put the leeks in a bowl and season to taste with salt and pepper. Let cool. Wash and dry the frying pan.

4 Divide the leeks among the chicken breasts, packing the pockets full. Secure the openings with wooden toothpicks.

5 Melt the remaining butter in the frying pan over medium high heat. Add the stuffed breasts and brown lightly on both sides.

6 Add the stock and bring to a boil. Cover and simmer for about 10 minutes, or until the chicken is cooked through. Carefully turn the breasts over halfway through the cooking.

7 With a slotted spatula, remove the breasts from the pan and keep warm. Boil the cooking liquid until it is reduced by half.

8 Stir the cream into the cooking liquid and boil until reduced by about half again. Stir in the lime juice and season to taste.

9 Remove the toothpicks from the breasts. Cut each breast on the diagonal into $^1/_2$-inch slices, pour the sauce over them and serve.

VARIATION

For Onion-stuffed Chicken Breasts, use 2 sweet onions, halved and thinly sliced, instead of leeks.

Pasta with Chicken Livers

Chicken livers in a piquant sauce served with pasta.

Serves 4

8 ounces chicken livers, defrosted
    if frozen
2 tablespoons olive oil
2 garlic cloves, crushed
6 ounces rindless Canadian bacon,
    coarsely chopped
14-ounce can chopped tomatoes
$2/3$ cup homemade or canned
    chicken stock
1 tablespoon tomato paste
1 tablespoon dry sherry
2 tablespoons chopped mixed fresh
    herbs, such as parsley, rosemary
    and basil
12 ounces dried orecchiette pasta
salt and black pepper
freshly grated Parmesan cheese, to serve

1 Wash and trim the chicken livers. Cut into bite-sized pieces. Heat the oil in a sauté pan and fry the chicken livers for 3–4 minutes, or until tender.

2 Add the garlic and bacon to the pan and fry until golden brown. Add the tomatoes, chicken stock, tomato paste, sherry, herbs and seasoning to taste.

3 Bring the sauce to the boil and simmer gently, uncovered, for about 5 minutes until the sauce has thickened. Stir from time to time.

4 Meanwhile, cook the pasta in boiling salted water for about 12 minutes until "al dente". Drain, then toss into the sauce. Serve hot, sprinkled with Parmesan cheese.

Chicken Baked in a Salt Crust

This unusual dish is extremely easy to make. Once it is cooked, you just break away the salt crust to reveal the wonderfully tender, golden brown chicken underneath.

Serves 4

1 corn-fed or free-range oven-ready
    chicken, 3–3$1/2$ pounds
bunch of mixed fresh herbs, such as
    rosemary, thyme, marjoram and parsley
7 cups coarse sea salt
1 egg white
1–2 whole heads of baked garlic,
    to serve

1 Preheat the oven to 350°F. Wipe the chicken. Put the herbs into the cavity, then truss the chicken.

2 Mix together the sea salt and egg white until all the salt crystals are moistened. Select a roasting pan into which the chicken will fit neatly, then line it with a large double layer of foil.

3 Spread a thick layer of the salt in the foil-lined pan and put the chicken on top. Cover with the remaining salt and shape neatly around the chicken, making sure it is completely enclosed.

4 Bring the foil edges up and over the chicken to enclose it and bake in the oven for 1$1/2$ hours. Remove from the oven and let rest for 10 minutes.

5 Carefully lift the foil package from the pan and open. Break the salt crust and brush any traces of salt from the bird. Serve with baked whole heads of garlic. Slip each clove from its skin and eat with a bite of chicken.

Risotto with Chicken

This is a complete meal cooked conveniently all in one pan.

Serves 4

2 tablespoons olive oil

8 ounces chicken breast, skinned, boned
   and cut into 1-inch cubes

1 onion, finely chopped

1 garlic clove, finely chopped

$^1/_4$ teaspoon saffron strands

$^1/_2$ cup Parma ham, cut
   into thin strips

2 cups risotto rice,
   preferably Arborio

$^1/_2$ cup dry white wine

$7^1/_2$ cups simmering chicken stock,
   preferably homemade

2 tablespoons butter (optional)

$^1/_3$ cup freshly grated Parmesan cheese,
   plus more to serve

salt and pepper

1 Heat the oil in a wide heavy-bottomed pan over medium high heat. Add the chicken cubes and cook, stirring, until they start to turn white.

2 Reduce the heat to low. Add the onion, garlic, saffron and Parma ham. Cook, stirring, until the onion is soft. Stir in the risotto rice and mix well. Sauté for 1–2 minutes, stirring constantly.

3 Add the wine and bring to a boil. Simmer gently until almost all the wine is absorbed.

4 Add the simmering stock, a ladleful at a time, and cook, stirring constantly, until the rice is just tender and the risotto creamy.

5 Add the butter, if using, and Parmesan cheese and stir in well. Season with salt and pepper to taste. Serve the risotto hot, sprinkled with more Parmesan.

Cannelloni al Forno

A lighter alternative to the usual beef-filled, béchamel-coated version. Fill with ricotta, onions and mushrooms for a vegetarian recipe.

INGREDIENTS

Serves 4–6

4 cups skinned and boned chicken
    breast, cooked
2 ¹/₂ cups mushrooms
2 garlic cloves, crushed
2 tablespoons chopped fresh parsley
1 tablespoon chopped fresh tarragon
1 egg, beaten
fresh lemon juice
12–18 cannelloni tubes
2 cups homemade or canned
    tomato sauce
²/₃ cup freshly grated Parmesan cheese
salt and pepper
1 sprig fresh parsley, to garnish

1 Preheat the oven to 400°F. Place the chicken in a blender or food processor and blend until finely ground. Transfer to a bowl.

2 Place the mushrooms, garlic, parsley and tarragon in the food processor and blend until finely ground.

3 Beat the mushroom mixture into the chicken mixture thoroughly, then add the egg, salt and pepper and lemon juice to taste and mix well.

4 If necessary, cook the cannelloni in plenty of salted boiling water according to the instructions, then drain well on a clean dish towel.

5 Place the filling in a pastry bag fitted with a large plain nozzle. Use this to fill each tube of cannelloni, once they are cool enough to handle.

6 Lay the filled cannelloni tightly together in a single layer in a buttered shallow ovenproof dish. Spoon the tomato sauce over them and sprinkle with Parmesan cheese. Bake in the oven for 30 minutes, or until brown and bubbling. Serve garnished with a sprig of parsley.

Chicken and Curry Mayonnaise Sandwich

A very useful and appetizing way of using leftover pieces of chicken.

Serves 2

4 slices whole wheat bread

2 tablespoons softened butter

4 ounces cooked chicken, sliced

3 tablespoons Curry Mayonnaise

1 bunch watercress, trimmed

1 Spread the bread with butter and arrange the chicken over two of the slices.

2 Spread the Curry Mayonnaise over the chicken slices.

3 Arrange a few sprigs of watercress on top, cover with the remaining bread, press lightly together and cut in half.

CURRY MAYONNAISE

Makes about ²/₃ cup

¹/₂ cup mayonnaise

2 teaspoons concentrated bottled curry paste or good curry powder

¹/₂ teaspoon lemon juice

2 teaspoons sieved apricot jam

Combine all the ingredients thoroughly and chill until needed.

Oriental Chicken Sandwich

This filling is also good served in warmed pita bread, in which case cut the chicken into small cubes before marinating. Broil on skewers and serve warm.

INGREDIENTS

Serves 2

1 tablespoon soy sauce

1 teaspoon honey

1 teaspoon sesame oil

1 garlic clove, crushed

6 ounces chicken breast,
  boned and skinned

4 slices white bread

4 tablespoons peanut butter

2 tablespoons beansprouts

1 ounce red bell pepper, seeded
  and finely sliced

2 sprigs parsley, to garnish

1 Mix together the soy sauce, honey, sesame oil and garlic. Brush on the chicken breast.

2 Broil the chicken for 3–4 minutes on each side until cooked through, then slice thinly.

3 Spread two slices of the bread with some of the peanut butter.

4 Arrange the slices of chicken on top of the peanut butter.

5 Spread a little more peanut butter over the chicken.

6 Sprinkle on the beansprouts and red pepper and sandwich together with the remaining slices of bread. Cut in half, if desired.

Chicken and Shiitake Mushroom Pizza

The addition of shiitake mushrooms adds an earthy flavor to this colorful pizza, while fresh red chili gives a hint of spiciness.

INGREDIENTS

Serves 3–4

3 tablespoons olive oil

3 cups chicken breast fillets,
   skinned and cut into thin strips

1 bunch scallions, sliced

1 fresh red chili, seeded and chopped

1 red bell pepper, seeded and cut
   into thin strips

3 ounces fresh shiitake mushrooms,
   wiped and sliced

3–4 tablespoons chopped
   fresh cilantro

1 pizza crust, about 10–12 inches
   diameter

1 tablespoon chili oil

1¹/₄ cups mozzarella cheese

salt and black pepper

1 Preheat the oven to 425°F. Heat 2 tablespoons of the olive oil in a wok or large frying pan. Add the chicken, scallions, chili, pepper and mushrooms and stir-fry over high heat for 2–3 minutes, until the chicken is firm but still slightly pink in the center. Season with salt and pepper.

2 Pour off any excess oil, then set aside the chicken mixture until cool.

3 Stir the fresh cilantro into the chicken mixture.

4 Brush the pizza crust with the chili oil.

5 Spoon on the chicken mixture and drizzle on the remaining olive oil.

6 Grate the mozzarella and sprinkle on. Bake for 15–20 minutes, until crisp and golden. Serve immediately.

Smoked Chicken Pizza

These ingredients complement each other perfectly and make a really delicious topping.

INGREDIENTS

Serves 4

4 small pizza crusts, about 5 inches
   diameter

3 tablespoons olive oil

4 tablespoons sun-dried tomato paste

2 yellow bell peppers, seeded and cut
   into thin strips

6 ounces sliced smoked chicken
   or turkey, chopped

1¼ cups mozzarella cheese,
   cut into cubes

2 tablespoons chopped fresh basil

salt and black pepper

1 Preheat the oven to 425°F. Place the pizza crusts well apart on two greased baking sheets.

2 Brush the pizza crusts with 1 tablespoon of the oil, then brush generously with tomato paste.

3 Stir-fry the peppers in half the remaining oil for 3–4 minutes.

4 Arrange the chicken and peppers on top of the sun-dried tomato paste.

5 Sprinkle on the mozzarella and basil. Season to taste with salt and black pepper.

6 Drizzle on the remaining oil and bake in the oven for 15–20 minutes, until crisp and golden. Serve immediately.

Chicken and Avocado Pita Pizzas

Pita bread is used here to make quick crusts for a tasty pizza.

INGREDIENTS

Serves 4

8 plum tomatoes, quartered

3–4 tablespoons olive oil

1 large ripe avocado

8 pita bread rounds

6–7 slices of cooked chicken, chopped

1 onion, thinly sliced

2^1/$_2$ cups grated Cheddar cheese

2 tablespoons chopped fresh cilantro

salt and pepper

1 Preheat the oven to 450°F.

2 Place the quartered tomatoes in a baking dish. Drizzle with 1 tablespoon of the oil and season to taste. Bake for 30 minutes; do not stir.

3 Remove the baking dish from the oven and mash the tomatoes with a fork, removing the skins as you mash. Set aside.

4 Peel and pit the avocado. Cut into 16 thin slices.

5 Brush the edges of the pita breads with oil. Arrange the breads on two baking sheets.

6 Spread each pita with mashed tomato, almost to the edges.

7 Top each with 2 avocado slices. Sprinkle with the chicken, then add a few onion slices. Season to taste. Sprinkle on the cheese.

8 Place one sheet in the middle of the oven and bake until the cheese begins to melt, about 15–20 minutes. Sprinkle with half the cilantro and serve. Meanwhile, bake the second batch of pizzas, and serve them hot.

Chicken Breasts with Tomato-Corn Salsa

This hot tomato salsa is good with any broiled or grilled meats.

INGREDIENTS

Serves 4

4 chicken breast halves, about 6 ounces
   each, boned and skinned
2 tablespoons fresh lemon juice
2 tablespoons olive oil
2 teaspoons ground cumin
2 teaspoons dried oregano
1 tablespoon coarse black pepper
salt

For the salsa

1 fresh hot green chili pepper
1 pound tomatoes, seeded and chopped
$1^{1}/_{4}$ cups corn, freshly cooked or thawed
3 scallions, chopped
1 tablespoon chopped fresh parsley
2 tablespoons chopped fresh cilantro
2 tablespoons fresh lemon juice
3 tablespoons olive oil
1 teaspoon salt

1 With a mallet, pound the chicken breasts between two sheets of plastic wrap until thin.

2 In a shallow dish, combine the lemon juice, oil, cumin, oregano and pepper.

3 Add the chicken and turn to coat. Cover and let stand for at least 2 hours, or chill overnight.

4 To make the salsa, char the chili skin over a gas flame (or under the broiler.) Let cool for 5 minutes. Wearing rubber gloves, carefully rub off the charred skin. For a less hot flavor, discard the seeds.

5 Chop the chili very finely and place in a bowl. Add the rest of the salsa ingredients and mix well.

6 Remove the chicken from the marinade. Season lightly.

7 Heat a ridged broiler pan. Add the chicken breasts and cook until browned, about 3 minutes. Turn and cook the meat on the other side for 3–4 minutes more. Serve the chicken with the salsa.

Pan-fried Honey Chicken Drumsticks

The sweetness of the honey contrasts well with the lemon and soy sauce.

Serves 4

$1/2$ cup honey

juice of 1 lemon

2 tablespoons soy sauce

1 tablespoon sesame seeds

$1/2$ teaspoon fresh or dried thyme leaves

12 chicken drumsticks

$1/2$ teaspoon salt

$1/2$ teaspoon pepper

$3/4$ cup all-purpose flour

3 tablespoons butter or margarine

3 tablespoons vegetable oil

$1/2$ cup white wine

$1/2$ cup homemade or canned chicken stock

1 In a large bowl, combine the honey, lemon juice, soy sauce, sesame seeds and thyme. Add the chicken drumsticks and mix to coat them well. Let marinate in a cool place for 2 hours or more, turning occasionally.

2 Mix the salt, pepper and flour in a shallow bowl. Drain the drumsticks, reserving the marinade. Roll them in the seasoned flour to coat all over.

3 Heat the butter or margarine with the oil in a large frying pan. When hot and sizzling, add the drumsticks. Brown them on all sides. Reduce the heat to medium–low and cook until the chicken is done, 12–15 minutes.

4 Test the drumsticks with a fork; the juices should run clear. Remove the drumsticks to a serving platter and keep hot.

5 Pour off most of the fat from the pan. Add the wine, stock and reserved marinade and stir well to mix in the cooking juices on the bottom of the pan. Bring to a boil and simmer until reduced by half. Check and adjust the seasoning, then spoon the sauce over the drumsticks and serve.

Chicken Liver Stir-fry

The final sprinkling of lemon, parsley and garlic gives this dish a delightfully fresh flavor and a wonderful aroma.

INGREDIENTS

Serves 4

1 1/4 pounds chicken livers

6 tablespoons butter

6 ounces small portobello mushrooms

2 ounces chanterelle mushrooms

3 cloves garlic, finely chopped

2 shallots, finely chopped

2/3 cup medium sherry

3 fresh rosemary sprigs

grated rind of 1 lemon

2 tablespoons chopped fresh parsley

salt and black pepper

rosemary sprigs, to garnish

4 thick slices of white toast, to serve

1 Clean and trim the chicken livers to remove any gristle, muscle or discolored bits.

2 Season the chicken livers generously with salt and ground black pepper, tossing well to coat them all thoroughly.

3 Heat a wok or large frying pan and add 1 tablespoon of the butter. When melted, add the livers in batches (melting more butter when necessary but reserving 2 tablespoons for the vegetables) and fast-fry until golden brown. Drain, using a slotted spoon, and transfer to a plate, then place in a low oven to keep warm.

4 Cut the portobello mushrooms into thick slices. If large, cut the chanterelles in half.

5 Heat the wok and add the remaining butter. Stir in two-thirds of the chopped garlic and the shallots and stir-fry for 1 minute, until golden brown. Stir in the mushrooms and continue to cook for another 2 minutes.

6 Add the sherry, bring to a boil and simmer for 2–3 minutes, until syrupy. Add the rosemary, seasoning and livers to the pan. Stir-fry for 1 minute. Garnish with the rosemary, and sprinkle with a mixture of lemon, parsley and the remaining chopped garlic. Serve with slices of toast.

ONE POT
MEALS

Nasi Goreng

This dish is originally from Thailand and can be easily adapted by adding any cooked ingredients you have on hand. Crisp shrimp crackers make an ideal accompaniment.

INGREDIENTS

Serves 4

1 cup long-grain rice

2 eggs

2 tablespoons vegetable oil

1 green chili

2 scallions, coarsely chopped

2 cloves garlic, crushed

8 ounces cooked chicken

8 ounces cooked shrimp

3 tablespoons dark soy sauce

shrimp crackers, to serve

1 Rinse the rice and then cook for 10–12 minutes in 2 cups water in a pan with a tight-fitting lid. When cooked, refresh under cold water.

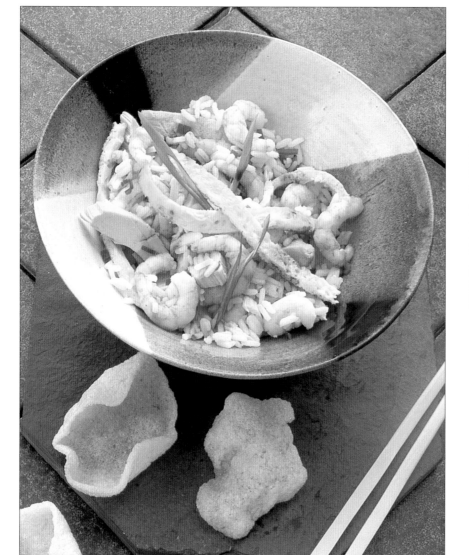

2 Lightly beat the eggs. Heat 1 tablespoon of oil in a small frying pan and swirl in the beaten egg. When cooked on one side, flip the egg over and cook on the other. Remove from the pan and let cool. Cut the omelet into strips.

3 Carefully remove the seeds from the chili and chop finely, wearing rubber gloves to protect your hands, if necessary. Place the scallions, chili and garlic in a blender or food processor and blend to a paste.

4 Heat the wok, and then add the remaining oil. When the oil is hot, add the chili paste and stir-fry for 1 minute.

5 Stir the chicken and shrimp into the chili paste.

6 Add the rice and stir-fry for 3–4 minutes. Stir in the soy sauce and serve with shrimp crackers.

Chicken and Rice Vermicelli

This delicious dish makes a filling meal. Take care when frying vermicelli, as it has a tendency to spit when added to hot oil.

INGREDIENTS

Serves 4

$^1/_2$ cup vegetable oil

8 ounces rice vermicelli

5 ounces green beans, ends removed and halved lengthwise

1 onion, finely chopped

2 chicken breasts, about 6 ounces each, boned, skinned and cut into strips

1 teaspoon cayenne pepper

8 ounces cooked shrimp

3 tablespoons dark soy sauce

3 tablespoons white wine vinegar

2 teaspoons sugar

cilantro sprigs, to garnish

1 Heat a wok or frying pan, then add 4 tablespoons of the oil. Break up the vermicelli into 3-inch lengths. When the oil is hot, fry the vermicelli in batches. Remove from the heat and keep warm.

2 Heat the remaining oil, then add the green beans, chopped onion and chicken and stir-fry for 3 minutes, until the chicken strips are cooked.

3 Sprinkle in the cayenne pepper. Stir in the cooked shrimp, soy sauce, vinegar and sugar, and stir-fry for 2 minutes.

4 Serve the chicken, shrimp and vegetables on the fried vermicelli, garnished with sprigs of cilantro.

Italian Chicken

Sun-dried tomatoes and pesto are a winning combination in this dish.

INGREDIENTS

Serves 4

2 tablespoons all-purpose flour

4 chicken portions (legs, breasts or
  quarters), skinned

2 tablespoons olive oil

1 onion, chopped

2 garlic cloves, chopped

1 red bell pepper, seeded and chopped

14-ounce can chopped tomatoes

2 tablespoons red pesto sauce

4 sun-dried tomatoes in oil, chopped

$2/3$ cup homemade or canned
  chicken stock

1 teaspoon dried oregano

8 black olives, pitted

salt and black pepper

chopped fresh basil and a few basil leaves,
  to garnish

tagliatelle, to serve

1 Place the flour and seasoning in a plastic bag. Add the chicken pieces and shake well until coated. Heat the oil in a flame-proof casserole, add the chicken and brown quickly. Remove with a spoon and set aside.

2 Lower the heat and add the onion, garlic and red pepper and cook for 5 minutes.

3 Stir in remaining ingredients, except the olives, and bring to a boil. Return the sautéed chicken to the casserole, season, cover and simmer for 30–35 minutes, or until the chicken is cooked.

4 Add the olives and simmer for 5 minutes. Place in a warmed serving dish, sprinkle with the chopped basil and garnish with a few basil leaves. Serve with hot tagliatelle, tossed in butter.

Honey and Orange Glazed Chicken

This way of cooking chicken breasts is popular in America, Australia and Great Britain. It is ideal for an easy evening meal served with baked potatoes and salad.

INGREDIENTS

Serves 4

6 ounces boneless chicken breasts

1 tablespoon oil

4 scallions, chopped

1 garlic clove, crushed

3 tablespoons honey

4 tablespoons fresh orange juice

1 orange, peeled and segmented

2 tablespoons soy sauce

fresh lemon balm or flat leaf parsley, to
  garnish

baked potatoes and mixed salad, to serve

1 Preheat the oven to 375°F. Place the chicken breasts in a shallow roasting pan and set aside.

2 Heat the oil in a small pan, and fry the scallions and garlic for 2 minutes, until softened. Add the honey, orange juice, orange segments and soy sauce to the pan, stirring well until the honey has dissolved.

3 Pour the sauce over the chicken and bake, uncovered, for about 45 minutes, basting with the honey glaze once or twice, until the chicken is cooked. Garnish with the lemon balm or parsley and serve the chicken and its sauce with baked potatoes and a salad.

Louisiana Rice

A tasty meal of pork, rice, chicken livers and an array of spices.

Serves 4

4 tablespoons vegetable oil

1 small eggplant, diced

8 ounces ground pork

1 green bell pepper, seeded and chopped

2 stalks celery, chopped

1 onion, chopped

1 garlic clove, crushed

1 teaspoon cayenne pepper

1 teaspoon paprika

1 teaspoon black pepper

$1/2$ teaspoon salt

1 teaspoon dried thyme

$1/2$ teaspoon dried oregano

2 cups homemade or canned
   chicken stock

8 ounces chicken livers, minced

$3/4$ cup long-grain rice

1 bay leaf

3 tablespoons chopped fresh parsley

celery leaves, to garnish

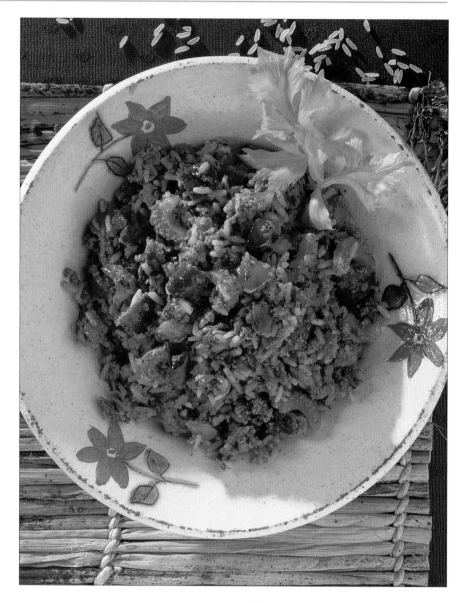

1 Heat the oil in a frying pan until really hot, then add the diced eggplant and stir-fry for about 5 minutes.

2 Add the pork and cook for about 6–8 minutes, until browned, using a wooden spoon to break any lumps.

3 Add the chopped green pepper, celery, onion, garlic and all the spices and herbs. Cover and cook over high heat for 5–6 minutes, stirring frequently from the bottom to scrape up and distribute the crispy brown bits.

4 Pour on the chicken stock and stir to clean the bottom of the pan. Cover and cook for 6 minutes over medium heat. Stir in the chicken livers, cook for 2 minutes, then stir in the rice and add the bay leaf.

5 Reduce the heat, cover and simmer for about 6–7 minutes. Turn off the heat and let stand for another 10–15 minutes, until the rice is tender. Remove the bay leaf and stir in the chopped parsley. Serve the rice hot, garnished with the celery leaves.

Chinese Special Fried Rice

Cooked white rice fried with a selection of other ingredients is a staple Chinese dish. This recipe combines a mixture of chicken, shrimp and vegetables with fried rice.

INGREDIENTS

Serves 4

1 cup long-grain white rice

3 tablespoons peanut oil

1 garlic clove, crushed

4 scallions, finely chopped

1 cup diced cooked chicken

1 cup cooked peeled shrimp
  (rinsed if canned)

1/2 cup frozen peas

1 egg, beaten with a pinch of salt

1 cup shredded lettuce

2 tablespoons light soy sauce

pinch of sugar

salt and black pepper

1 tablespoon chopped roasted cashews, to
  garnish

1 Rinse the long-grain rice in two to three changes of warm water to wash away some of the starch. Drain well.

2 Put the rice in a saucepan and add 1 tablespoon of the oil and 1 1/2 cups of water. Cover and bring to a boil, stir once, then cover and simmer for 12–15 minutes, until nearly all the water has been absorbed. Turn off the heat and let stand covered for 10 minutes. Fluff rice with a fork and let cool, uncovered.

3 Heat the remaining oil in a wok or frying pan, add the garlic and scallions and stir-fry for 30 seconds.

4 Add the chicken, shrimp and peas and stir-fry for 1–2 minutes, then add the cooked rice and stir-fry for another 2 minutes. Pour in the egg and stir-fry until just set. Stir in the lettuce, soy sauce, sugar and seasoning.

5 Transfer to a warmed serving bowl, sprinkle with the chopped roasted cashews and serve immediately.

Chicken Teriyaki

Boiled rice is the ideal accompaniment to this Japanese-style dish.

INGREDIENTS

Serves 4

1 pound chicken breasts, boned and
　skinned
orange segments, mustard greens and
　watercress, to garnish

For the marinade
1 teaspoon sugar
1 tablespoon rice wine
1 tablespoon dry sherry
2 tablespoons dark soy sauce
rind of 1 orange, grated

1 Slice the chicken breasts into thin strips. Mix all the marinade ingredients in a bowl.

2 Place the chicken in a bowl, pour on the marinade and let marinate for 15 minutes.

3 Heat a wok or large frying pan, add the chicken and marinade and stir-fry for 4–5 minutes. Serve the chicken garnished with orange segments and the greens.

COOK'S TIP

Make sure the marinade is brought to a boil and cooked for 4–5 minutes, because it has been in contact with raw chicken.

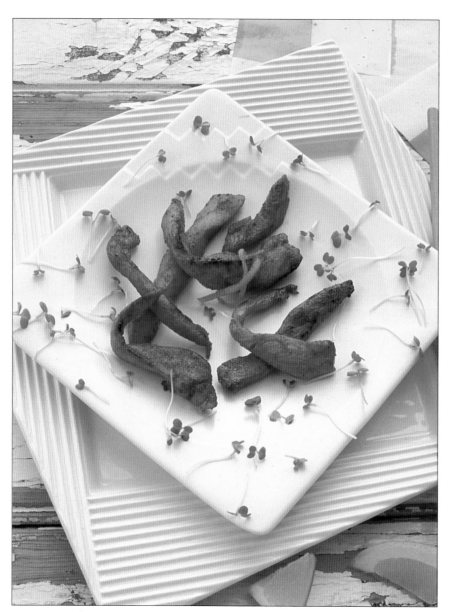

Thai Fried Noodles

Pork, chicken and fish stir-fried with noodles and lime juice.

Serves 4

8 ounces thread egg noodles

4 tablespoons vegetable oil

2 garlic cloves, finely chopped

6 ounces pork tenderloin,
   sliced into thin strips

1 chicken breast, about 6 ounces, boned,
   skinned and sliced into thin strips

1 cup cooked peeled shrimps
   (rinsed if canned)

3 tablespoons lime or lemon juice

3 tablespoons Thai fish sauce

2 tablespoons light brown sugar

2 eggs, beaten

$1/2$ red chili, seeded and finely chopped

$1/4$ cup beansprouts

4 tablespoons roasted peanuts, chopped

3 scallions, cut into 2-inch lengths
   and shredded

3 tablespoons chopped fresh cilantro

1 Place the noodles in a large pan of boiling water and let stand for about 5 minutes.

2 Meanwhile, heat 3 tablespoons of the oil in a wok or large frying pan, add the garlic and cook for 30 seconds. Add the pork and chicken and stir-fry over high heat until lightly browned, then add the shrimp, and stir-fry for 2 minutes.

3 Add the lime or lemon juice, fish sauce and sugar and stir-fry until the sugar has dissolved.

4 Drain the noodles and add to the pan with the remaining 1 tablespoon oil. Toss all the ingredients together.

5 Pour on the beaten eggs. Stir-fry until almost set, then add the chili and beansprouts. Divide the peanuts, scallions and cilantro leaves into two and add half to the pan. Stir-fry for 2 minutes, then tip on to a serving platter. Sprinkle on the remaining peanuts, scallions and cilantro and serve at once.

Chicken and Shrimp Jambalaya

The mixture of chicken, seafood and rice suggests a close relationship to the Spanish paella, but the name is probably derived from jambon (French for ham) and à la ya (Creole for rice). Jambalayas are a colorful mixture of highly flavored ingredients, and are always made in large quantities for big family or celebration meals.

INGREDIENTS

Serves 10

2 chickens, 3 pounds each

1 pound piece raw smoked ham

4 tablespoons crisco or bacon fat

$^1/_2$ cup all-purpose flour

3 medium onions, finely sliced

2 green bell peppers,
   seeded and sliced

1$^1/_2$ pounds tomatoes, skinned and
   chopped

2–3 garlic cloves, crushed

2 teaspoons chopped fresh thyme
   or 1 teaspoon dried thyme

24 cooked large shrimp, heads removed
   and peeled

3 cups long-grain rice

2–3 dashes Tabasco sauce

1 bunch scallions, finely chopped
   (including the green parts)

3 tablespoons chopped fresh parsley

salt and black pepper

COOK'S TIP

The roux thickening is a vital part of Cajun cooking, particularly essential to jambalaya. Cook the roux over low heat, watching like a hawk so that it doesn't develop dark flecks, which indicate burning. Don't stop stirring for an instant.

1 Cut each chicken into 10 pieces and season with salt and pepper.

2 Dice the ham, discarding the rind and fat.

3 In a large heavy-bottomed pan melt the lard or bacon fat and brown the chicken pieces all over, lifting them out with a slotted spoon and setting them aside as they are done.

4 Turn the heat down, sprinkle the flour onto the fat in the pan and stir continuously until the roux turns light golden brown (see Cook's Tip below).

5 Return the chicken pieces to the pan, add the diced ham, onions, green peppers, tomatoes, garlic and thyme and cook, stirring often, for 10 minutes, then stir in the shrimp.

6 Stir the rice into the pan with one-and-a-half times the rice's volume in cold water. Season with salt, pepper and Tabasco sauce. Bring to a boil and cook over gentle heat until the rice is tender and the liquid absorbed. Add a little extra boiling water if the rice looks like it is drying out before it is cooked.

7 Mix the scallions and parsley into the finished dish, reserving a little of the mixture to sprinkle over the jambalaya as a garnish. Serve hot.

Burgundy Chicken

A dinner-party classic, perfect with a good bottle of red wine.

INGREDIENTS

Serves 4

4 tablespoons all-purpose flour

1 chicken, 3 pounds, cut into 8 pieces

1 tablespoon olive oil

5 tablespoons butter

20 baby onions

3 ounces piece lean bacon without rind, diced

about 20 button mushrooms

1 bottle red Burgundy wine

bouquet garni

3 garlic cloves

1 teaspoon light brown sugar

salt and black pepper

1 tablespoon chopped fresh parsley and croutons, to garnish

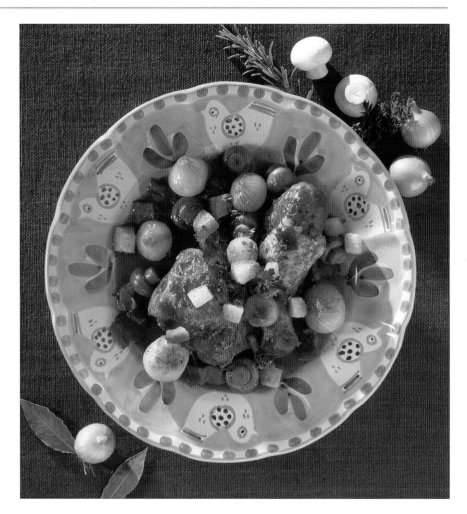

1 Place 3 tablespoons of the flour and the seasoning in a large plastic bag and shake each chicken piece in it until lightly coated. Heat the oil and 4 tablespoons of the butter in a large flameproof casserole. Add the onions and bacon and sauté for 3–4 minutes, until the onions have lightly browned. Add the mushrooms and fry for 2 minutes. Remove with a slotted spoon into a bowl and reserve.

2 Add the chicken pieces to the hot oil and cook until browned on all sides, about 5–6 minutes. Pour on the Burgundy wine and add the bouquet garni, garlic, light brown sugar and seasoning.

3 Bring to a boil, cover and simmer for 1 hour, stirring occasionally.

4 Return the reserved onions, bacon and mushrooms to the casserole, cover and cook for another 30 minutes.

5 Lift out the cooked chicken, vegetables and bacon with a slotted spoon and arrange on a warmed dish. Remove the bouquet garni and boil the liquid rapidly for 2 minutes to reduce slightly. Cream the remaining butter and flour together and whisk in teaspoonfuls of the mixture until thickened slightly. Pour over the chicken and garnish with parsley and croutons.

Apricot and Chicken Casserole

A mild curried and fruity chicken dish served with almond rice. Makes a good winter meal.

INGREDIENTS

Serves 4

1 tablespoon oil

8 chicken thighs, boned and skinned

1 medium onion, finely chopped

1 teaspoon medium curry powder

2 tablespoons all-purpose flour

$1^7/8$ cups homemade or canned
  chicken stock

juice of 1 large orange

8 dried apricots, halved

1 tablespoon golden raisins

salt and black pepper

For the almond rice

2 cups cooked long-grain rice

1 tablespoon butter

$^1/2$ cup toasted, slivered almonds

1 Preheat the oven to 375°F. Heat the oil in a large frying pan. Cut the chicken into cubes and brown quickly all over in the oil. Add the chopped onion and cook gently until soft and lightly browned.

2 Transfer the chicken and onion to a large flameproof casserole, sprinkle in the curry powder and cook again for a few minutes. Add the flour and blend in the stock and orange juice. Bring to a boil and season with salt and freshly ground black pepper.

3 Add the apricots and golden raisins, cover with a lid and cook gently for an hour, or until tender, in the preheated oven. Adjust the seasoning to taste.

4 To make the almond rice, reheat the pre-cooked rice with the butter and season to taste. Stir in the toasted almonds just before serving.

Chicken in Creamed Horseradish

The piquant flavor of horseradish sauce gives this quick dish a sophisticated taste. Use half the quantity if using fresh horseradish.

INGREDIENTS

Serves 4

2 tablespoons olive oil

4 chicken pieces

2 tablespoons butter

2 tablespoons all-purpose flour

1⁷/₈ cups homemade or canned
   chicken stock

2 tablespoons bottled horseradish sauce

salt and black pepper

1 tablespoon chopped fresh parsley, to
   garnish

mashed potatoes and tender green
   beans, to serve

1 Heat the oil in a large flame-proof casserole and gently brown the chicken pieces on both sides over medium heat. Remove the chicken from the casserole and keep warm.

2 Wipe out the casserole, melt the butter, stir in the flour and blend in the stock gradually. Bring to a boil, stirring all the time.

3 Add the horseradish sauce and season with salt and freshly ground black pepper. Return the chicken to the casserole, cover and simmer for 30–40 minutes, or until the chicken is tender.

4 Transfer to a serving dish and sprinkle with fresh parsley. Serve with mashed potatoes and green beans, if desired.

Chicken Paella

There are many variations of this basic recipe. Any seasonal vegetables can be added, together with mussels and other shellfish. Serve right from the pan.

Serves 4

4 chicken legs (thighs and drumsticks)

4 tablespoons olive oil

1 large onion, finely chopped

1 garlic clove, crushed

1 teaspoon ground turmeric

4 ounces chorizo sausage or smoked ham

1 cup long-grain rice

2^1/$_2$ cups homemade or canned
   chicken stock

4 tomatoes, skinned, seeded and chopped

1 red bell pepper, seeded and sliced

1 cup frozen peas

salt and black pepper

1 Preheat the oven to 350°F. Cut the chicken legs in half.

2 Heat the oil in a 12-inch paella pan or large flameproof casserole and brown the chicken pieces on both sides. Add the onion and garlic and stir in the turmeric. Cook for 2 minutes.

3 Slice the sausage or dice the ham and add to the pan, with the rice and stock. Bring to a boil and season to taste; cover and bake for 15 minutes.

4 Remove from the oven and add the chopped tomatoes, sliced red pepper and frozen peas. Return to the oven and cook for another 10–15 minutes, or until the chicken is tender and the rice has absorbed the stock.

Chicken with Bell Peppers

This colorful dish comes from the south of Italy, where sweet peppers are plentiful.

INGREDIENTS

Serves 4

1 chicken, 3 pounds, cut into
    serving pieces

3 large bell peppers, red, yellow or green

6 tablespoons olive oil

2 medium red onions, finely sliced

2 cloves garlic, finely chopped

small piece of dried chili, crumbled
    (optional)

$1/2$ cup white wine

salt and black pepper

2 tomatoes, fresh or canned, peeled and
    chopped

3 tablespoons chopped fresh parsley

1 Trim any fat off the chicken, and remove all excess skin. Prepare peppers by cutting them in half and discarding the seeds and the stem. Slice into strips.

2 Heat half the oil in a large heavy saucepan or casserole. Add the onions, and cook over low heat until soft. Remove to a side dish. Add the remaining oil to the pan, raise the heat to medium, add the chicken and brown on all sides, 6–8 minutes. Return the onions to the pan, and add the garlic and dried chili, if using.

3 Pour in the wine, and cook until it has reduced by half. Add the peppers and stir well to coat them with the oil. Season. After 3–4 minutes, stir in the tomatoes. Lower the heat, cover the pan, and cook until the peppers are soft, and the chicken is cooked, about 25–30 minutes. Stir occasionally. Stir in the chopped parsley and serve.

Chicken Breasts Cooked in Butter

This simple and very delicious way of cooking chicken brings out all of its delicacy.

INGREDIENTS

Serves 4

4 small chicken breasts, skinned
    and boned

flour seasoned with salt and freshly
    ground black pepper, for dredging

6 tablespoons butter

1 sprig fresh parsley, to garnish

1 Separate the two fillets of each breast. They come apart very easily; one is large, the other small. Pound the large fillets between two sheets of plastic wrap lightly to flatten them. Dredge the chicken in the seasoned flour, shaking off any excess.

2 Heat the butter in a large heavy frying pan until it bubbles. Place all the chicken fillets in the pan, in one layer if possible. Cook over medium to high heat for 3–4 minutes, until they are golden brown.

3 Turn the chicken over. Reduce the heat to low to medium, and continue cooking until the fillets are cooked through but still springy to the touch, about 9–12 minutes in all. If the chicken begins to brown too much, cover the pan for the final minutes of cooking. Serve immediately garnished with a little parsley.

Chicken in Green Sauce

Slow, gentle cooking makes the chicken succulent and tender.

INGREDIENTS

Serves 4

2 tablespoons butter

1 tablespoon olive oil

4 chicken portions

1 small onion, finely chopped

$^2/_3$ cup medium dry white wine

$^2/_3$ cup homemade or canned
  chicken stock

6 ounces watercress

2 thyme sprigs and 2 tarragon sprigs

$^2/_3$ cup heavy cream

salt and black pepper

watercress leaves, to garnish

1 Heat the butter and oil in a heavy shallow pan, then brown the chicken evenly. Transfer the chicken to a plate, using a slotted spoon, and keep warm in the oven.

2 Add the onion to the cooking juices in the pan and cook until softened but not colored.

3 Stir in the wine, boil for 2–3 minutes, then add the stock and bring to a boil. Return the chicken to the pan, cover tightly and cook very gently for about 30 minutes, until the chicken juices run clear. Then transfer the chicken to a warm dish, cover the dish and keep warm.

4 Boil the cooking juices hard until reduced to about 4 tablespoons. Add the leaves from the watercress and herbs to the pan with the cream and simmer over medium heat until the sauce has thickened slightly.

5 Return the cooked chicken to the casserole, season and heat through for a few minutes. Garnish with watercress leaves before serving.

Stoved Chicken

"Stoved" is derived from the French étouffer – to cook in a covered pot – and originates from the seventeenth century.

INGREDIENTS

Serves 4

2¼ pounds potatoes,
   cut into ¼-inch slices
2 large onions, thinly sliced
1 tablespoon chopped fresh thyme
2 tablespoons butter
1 tablespoon oil
2 large slices bacon, chopped
4 large chicken quarters, halved
1 bay leaf
2½ cups homemade or canned
   chicken stock
salt and black pepper

1 Preheat the oven to 300°F. Make a thick layer of half the potato slices in the bottom of a large, heavy casserole, then cover with half the onion. Sprinkle with half the thyme, and salt and pepper.

2 Heat the butter and oil in a large frying pan, then brown the bacon and chicken.

3 Using a slotted spoon, transfer the chicken and bacon to the casserole. Reserve the fat in the pan. Sprinkle the remaining thyme, bay leaf and some seasoning over the chicken, then cover with the remaining onion, followed by a neat layer of overlapping potato slices. Sprinkle with seasoning.

4 Pour the stock into the casserole, brush the potatoes with the reserved fat, then cover tightly and cook in the oven for about 2 hours, until the chicken is tender.

5 Preheat the broiler. Uncover the casserole, place under the broiler and cook until the slices of potato are beginning to brown and crisp. Serve hot.

Parmesan Chicken Bake

The tomato sauce may be made the day before and left to cool. Serve with crusty bread and salad.

Serves 4

4 chicken breasts, boned and skinned

4 tablespoons all-purpose flour

4 tablespoons olive oil

salt and black pepper

For the tomato sauce

1 tablespoon olive oil

1 onion, finely chopped

1 stalk celery, finely chopped

1 red bell pepper, seeded and diced

1 garlic clove, crushed

14-ounce can chopped tomatoes with
   their juice

$2/3$ cup homemade/canned chicken stock

1 tablespoon tomato paste

2 teaspoons sugar

1 tablespoon chopped fresh basil

1 tablespoon chopped fresh parsley

To assemble

8 ounces mozzarella cheese, sliced

4 tablespoons grated Parmesan cheese

2 tablespoons fresh breadcrumbs

1 To make the tomato sauce, heat 1 tablespoon of the oil in a frying pan and gently cook the onion, celery, pepper and crushed garlic in the oil until tender.

2 Add the tomatoes with their juice, the stock, paste, sugar and herbs. Season to taste and bring to a boil. Simmer for 30 minutes to make a thick sauce, stirring occasionally.

3 Divide the chicken breasts into two natural fillets, place between sheets of plastic wrap and flatten to a thickness of $1/4$ inch with a rolling pin.

4 Season the flour. Toss the chicken breasts in the flour to coat, shaking to remove the excess.

5 Preheat the oven to 350°F. Heat the remaining oil in a large frying pan and cook the chicken quickly in batches for 3–4 minutes, until colored. Remove and keep warm while frying the rest of the chicken.

6 To assemble, layer the chicken pieces in a large baking dish with the cheeses and thick tomato sauce, finishing with a layer of cheese and breadcrumbs on top. Bake uncovered for 20–30 minutes or until golden brown.

Chicken with Mushrooms

*Serve on a dish surrounded with
nutty brown rice or tagliatelle verde.
White wine or brandy may be used
to deglaze the pan in place of sherry.*

INGREDIENTS

Serves 4

4 large chicken breasts, boned and skinned

3 tablespoons olive oil

1 onion, thinly sliced

1 garlic clove, crushed

3 cups button mushrooms,
   quartered

2 tablespoons sherry

1 tablespoon lemon juice

$^1/_3$ cup light cream

salt and black pepper

1 Divide the chicken breasts into
two natural fillets. Place each
between two sheets of plastic
wrap and flatten to a thickness of
$^1/_4$ inch with a rolling pin. Cut into
1-inch diagonal strips.

2 Heat 2 tablespoons of the oil in
a large frying pan and cook the
onion and crushed garlic slowly
until tender.

3 Add the mushrooms and cook
them for another 5 minutes.
Remove and keep warm.

4 Increase the heat. Add the
remaining oil and fry the
chicken very quickly, in small
batches, for 3–4 minutes, until
lightly colored. Season each batch
with a little salt and freshly ground
black pepper. Remove and keep
warm on a plate while frying the
rest of the chicken.

5 Add the sherry and lemon juice
to the pan and quickly return
the chicken, onions, garlic and
mushrooms, stirring to coat.

6 Stir in the cream and bring to a
boil. Adjust the seasoning to
taste. Serve immediately.

Chicken with White Wine and Garlic

Add the extra garlic to this dish if you like a stronger flavor.

INGREDIENTS

Serves 4

1 chicken, 3^1/$_2$ pounds,
    cut into serving pieces
1 onion, sliced
3–6 garlic cloves, to taste, crushed
1 teaspoon dried thyme
2 cups dry white wine
1 cup green olives (16–18),
    pitted
1 bay leaf
1 tablespoon lemon juice
1–2 tablespoons butter
salt and black pepper

1 Heat a deep, heavy frying pan. When hot, add the chicken pieces, skin side down, and cook over medium heat until browned, about 10 minutes. Turn and brown the other side, 5–8 minutes more.

2 Transfer the chicken pieces to a plate and set aside.

3 Drain the excess fat from the frying pan, leaving about 1 tablespoon. Add the sliced onion and ^{1}/$_2$ teaspoon salt and cook until just soft, about 5 minutes. Add the garlic and thyme and cook 1 minute more.

4 Add the wine and stir, scraping up any bits that cling to the pan. Bring to a boil and boil for 1 minute. Stir in the olives.

5 Return the chicken pieces to the pan. Add the bay leaf and season lightly with pepper. Lower the heat, cover, and simmer until the chicken is cooked through, about 20–30 minutes.

6 Transfer the chicken pieces to a warmed plate. Stir the lemon juice into the sauce. Whisk in the butter to thicken the sauce slightly. Spoon on top and serve.

Chicken Meat Loaf

Just slice the loaf up and serve it hot or cold.

INGREDIENTS

Serves 4

1 tablespoon olive oil
1 onion, chopped
1 green bell pepper, seeded and chopped
1 garlic clove, crushed
1 pound ground chicken
1 cup fresh breadcrumbs
1 egg, beaten
^{1}/$_2$ cup pine nuts
12 sun-dried tomatoes in oil, drained and
    chopped
5 tablespoons milk
2 teaspoons chopped fresh rosemary, or
    ^{1}/$_2$ teaspoon dried rosemary
1 teaspoon ground fennel seeds
^{1}/$_2$ teaspoon dried oregano
^{1}/$_2$ teaspoon salt

1 Preheat the oven to 375°F. Heat the oil in a frying pan. Add the onion, green pepper and garlic and cook over low heat, stirring often, until just softened, about 8–10 minutes. Remove from the heat and allow to cool.

2 Place the chicken in a large bowl. Add the onion mixture and the remaining ingredients and mix thoroughly.

3 Transfer to an 8^1/$_2$ x 4^1/$_2$-inch loaf tin, packing the mixture down firmly. Bake until golden brown, about 1 hour. Serve hot or cold in slices.

French-style Pot Roast Rock Cornish Hens

An incredibly simple dish that looks and tastes extra special.

INGREDIENTS

Serves 4

1 tablespoon olive oil

1 onion, sliced

1 large garlic clove, sliced

$^1/_2$ cup diced lightly smoked bacon

2 fresh Rock Cornish hens, just under
   1 pound each

2 tablespoons melted butter

2 baby celery hearts, each cut into 4 pieces

8 baby carrots

2 small zucchini, cut into chunks

8 small new potatoes

$2^1/_2$ cups homemade or canned
   chicken stock

$^2/_3$ cup dry white wine

1 bay leaf

2 fresh thyme sprigs

2 fresh rosemary sprigs

1 tablespoon butter, softened

1 tablespoon all-purpose flour

salt and black pepper

fresh herbs, to garnish

1 Preheat the oven to 375°F. Heat the olive oil in a large flame-proof casserole and add the onion, garlic and bacon. Sauté for 5–6 minutes, until the onion has softened.

2 Brush the birds with a little melted butter and season well. Lay birds on top of the onion mixture with the vegetables around. Add the chicken stock, wine and herbs.

3 Cover, bake for 20 minutes, then remove the lid and brush the birds with the remaining melted butter. Bake for another 25–30 minutes, until golden.

4 Transfer the birds to a warmed serving platter and cut each in half with poultry shears or scissors. Remove the vegetables with a slotted spoon and arrange them around the birds. Cover with foil and keep warm.

5 Discard the herbs from the pan juices. In a bowl, mix the butter and flour to form a paste. Bring the liquid in the pan to a boil and then whisk in teaspoonfuls of the paste until thickened. Season the sauce and serve with the Rock Cornish hens and vegetables, garnished with fresh herbs.

Coq au Vin

There are many variations to this traditional French dish, but this one is especially delicious. Serve it with warm French bread.

Serves 4

2 tablespoons olive oil

2 tablespoons butter

1 chicken, 3^1/$_2$ pounds, cut into 8 pieces

4 ounces ham, cut into ^{1}/$_4$-inch strips

4 ounces baby onions, peeled

1^1/$_2$ cups button mushrooms

2 garlic cloves, crushed

2 tablespoons brandy

1 cup red wine

1^1/$_4$ cups homemade or canned
    chicken stock

1 bouquet garni

2 tablespoons butter, blended with
    2 tablespoons flour

salt and black pepper

chopped parsley, to garnish

1 Preheat the oven to 325°F. Heat the oil and butter in a large flameproof casserole and brown the chicken pieces on all sides.

2 Add the ham strips, peeled onions, mushrooms and crushed garlic.

3 Pour in the brandy and light it. When the flames have subsided, add the red wine, stock, bouquet garni and seasoning. Cover and cook slowly for about 1 hour in the preheated oven.

4 Remove the chicken and keep warm. Thicken the sauce with the butter mixture and season to taste. Cook for several minutes and replace the chicken. Sprinkle with chopped parsley and serve.

Chicken in Creamy Orange Sauce

This sauce is deceptively creamy – in fact, it is made with low-fat ricotta cheese, which is virtually fat-free. The brandy adds a rich flavor, but is optional – omit it if you wish and use orange juice alone.

INGREDIENTS

Serves 4

8 chicken thighs or drumsticks, skinned

3 tablespoons brandy

1¼ cups orange juice

3 scallions, chopped

2 teaspoons cornstarch

⅓ cup low-fat ricotta cheese

salt and black pepper

rice or pasta and green salad, to serve

1 Fry the chicken pieces without fat in a nonstick or heavy pan, turning until evenly browned.

2 Stir in the brandy, orange juice and scallions. Bring to a boil, then cover and simmer for 15 minutes, or until the chicken is tender and the juices run clear, not pink, when pierced.

3 Blend the cornstarch with a little water, then mix into the ricotta. Stir this into the sauce and stir over medium heat until boiling.

4 Adjust the seasoning and serve with boiled rice or pasta and green salad.

COOK'S TIP

Cornstarch helps to stabilize the ricotta cheese and stop it from curdling.

Tuscan Chicken

This simple peasant casserole has all the flavors of traditional Tuscan food. The wine can be replaced by chicken stock.

INGREDIENTS

Serves 4

8 chicken thighs, skinned

1 teaspoon olive oil

1 medium onion, thinly sliced

2 red bell peppers, seeded and sliced

1 garlic clove, crushed

$1^1/_4$ cups puréed tomatoes

$^2/_3$ cup dry white wine

large sprig fresh oregano, or 1 teaspoon dried oregano

14-ounce can cannellini beans, drained

3 tablespoons fresh breadcrumbs

salt and black pepper

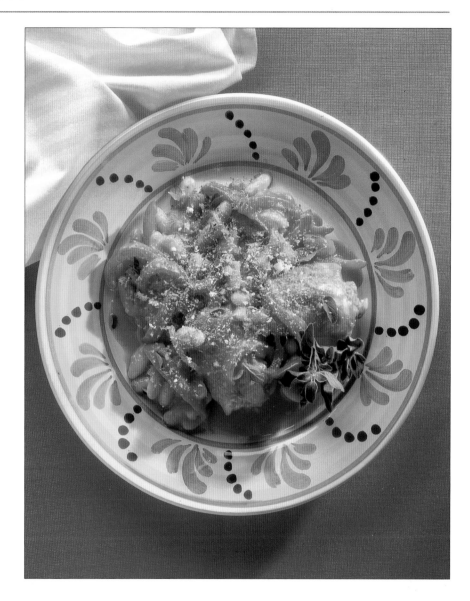

1 Fry the chicken in the oil in a nonstick or heavy pan until golden brown. Remove and keep hot. Add the onion and peppers to the pan and gently sauté until softened, but not brown. Stir in the garlic.

2 Add the chicken, puréed tomatoes, wine and oregano. Season well, bring to a boil, then cover the pan tightly.

3 Lower the heat and simmer gently, stirring occasionally, for 30–35 minutes, or until the chicken is tender and the juices run clear, not pink, when pierced with the point of a knife.

4 Stir in the cannellini beans and simmer for another 5 minutes until heated through. Sprinkle with the breadcrumbs and cook under a hot broiler until golden brown.

Koftas in Tomato Sauce

Delicious meatballs in a rich tomato sauce. Serve with pasta and grated Parmesan cheese, if desired.

INGREDIENTS

Serves 4

1¹/₂ pounds chicken
1 onion, grated
1 garlic clove, crushed
1 tablespoon chopped fresh parsley
¹/₂ teaspoon ground cumin
¹/₂ teaspoon ground coriander
1 egg, beaten
seasoned flour, for rolling
¹/₄ cup olive oil
salt and black pepper
chopped fresh parsley, to garnish

For the tomato sauce

1 tablespoon butter
2 tablespoons all-purpose flour
1 cup homemade or canned chicken stock
14-ounce can chopped tomatoes, with
    their juice
1 teaspoon sugar
¹/₄ teaspoon dried mixed herbs

1 Preheat the oven to 350°F. Remove any skin and bone from the chicken and grind or chop finely.

2 Put into a bowl together with the onion, garlic, parsley, spices, seasoning and beaten egg.

3 Mix thoroughly and shape into 1¹/₂-inch balls. Roll lightly in seasoned flour.

4 Heat the oil in a frying pan and brown the balls in small batches (this keeps the oil temperature hot and prevents the flour from becoming soggy). Remove and drain on paper towels. There is no need to cook the balls any longer at this stage, as they will cook in the tomato sauce.

5 To make the tomato sauce, melt the butter in a large saucepan. Add the flour, and then blend in the stock and tomatoes along with their juice. Add the sugar and mixed herbs. Bring to a boil, cover and simmer for 10–15 minutes.

6 Place the browned chicken balls into a shallow ovenproof dish and pour on the tomato sauce, cover with foil and bake in the preheated oven for 30–40 minutes. Adjust the seasoning to taste and sprinkle with parsley.

Spanish Chicken

A colorful one pot dish, ideal for entertaining and delicious served with a crisp green salad.

INGREDIENTS

Serves 8

2 tablespoons all-purpose flour

2 teaspoons ground paprika

$1/2$ teaspoon salt

16 chicken drumsticks

$1/4$ cup olive oil

5 cups homemade or canned
   chicken stock

1 onion, finely chopped

2 garlic cloves, crushed

$2^2/3$ cups long-grain rice

2 bay leaves

$1^1/3$ cups diced cooked ham

1 cup pimento-stuffed green olives

1 green bell pepper, seeded and diced

14-ounce cans chopped tomatoes, with
   their juice

4 tablespoons chopped fresh parsley

1 Preheat the oven to 350°F. Shake together the flour, paprika and salt in a plastic bag, add the drumsticks and toss to coat.

2 Heat the oil in a large flame-proof casserole and, working in batches, brown the chicken drumsticks slowly on all sides. Remove and keep warm.

3 Meanwhile, bring the stock to a boil and add the onion, crushed garlic, rice and bay leaves. Cook for 10 minutes. Add the ham, olives, pepper, and canned tomatoes with their juice. Mix well and transfer to a shallow ovenproof dish.

4 Arrange the chicken on top, cover and bake for 30–40 minutes, or until tender. Add a little more stock, if necessary, to prevent it from drying out. Remove the bay leaves and sprinkle on the chopped parsley to garnish.

Chicken with Lemon and Herbs

The herbs can be changed according to what is available; for example, parsley or thyme could be used instead of tarragon and fennel.

INGREDIENTS

Serves 2

4 tablespoons butter

2 scallions, white part only, finely chopped

1 tablespoon chopped fresh tarragon

1 tablespoon chopped fresh fennel

juice of 1 lemon

4 chicken thighs

salt and black pepper

lemon slices and herb sprigs, to garnish

1 Preheat the broiler to medium. In a small saucepan, melt the butter, then add the scallions, herbs, lemon juice and seasoning.

2 Brush the chicken generously with the herb mixture, then broil for 10–12 minutes, basting frequently with the herb mixture.

3 Turn over and baste again, then cook for another 10–12 minutes, or until the chicken juices run clear.

4 Serve garnished with lemon and herbs and with any remaining herb mixture.

Chicken with Red Cabbage

Chestnuts and red cabbage make a colorful winter dish.

INGREDIENTS

Serves 4

4 tablespoons butter

4 large chicken portions, halved

1 onion, chopped

1$^{1}/_{4}$ pounds red cabbage, finely shredded

4 juniper berries, crushed

12 cooked peeled chestnuts

$^{1}/_{2}$ cup full-bodied red wine

salt and black pepper

1 Heat the butter in a heavy flameproof casserole and lightly brown the chicken pieces. Transfer to a plate.

2 Add the onion to the casserole and fry gently until soft and light golden brown. Stir the cabbage and juniper berries into the casserole, season and cook over medium heat for 6–7 minutes, stirring once or twice.

3 Stir the chestnuts into the casserole, then tuck the chicken pieces under the cabbage so they are on the bottom of the casserole. Pour in the red wine.

4 Cover and cook gently for about 40 minutes, until the chicken juices run clear and the cabbage is very tender. Check the seasoning and serve.

Chicken with Blackberries and Lemon

This delicious stew combines some wonderful flavors. The red wine and blackberries give it a dramatic appearance.

INGREDIENTS

Serves 4

4 partly boned chicken breasts

2 tablespoons butter

1 tablespoon sunflower oil

4 tablespoons all-purpose flour

$2/3$ cup red wine

$2/3$ cup homemade or canned chicken stock

grated rind of $1/2$ orange, plus 1 tablespoon juice

3 sprigs lemon balm, finely chopped, plus 1 sprig to garnish

$2/3$ cup heavy cream

1 egg yolk

1 cup fresh blackberries, plus $1/2$ cup to garnish

salt and black pepper

1 Preheat the oven to 350°F. Remove any skin from the chicken, and season the meat. Heat the butter and oil in a frying pan, fry the chicken until golden, then transfer to a casserole dish. Stir the flour into the pan, then add the wine and stock and bring to a boil. Add the orange rind and juice, and the chopped lemon balm. Pour over the chicken.

2 Cover the casserole and cook in the oven for about 40 minutes.

3 Blend the cream with the egg yolk, add some of the liquid from the casserole and stir back into the dish with the blackberries (reserving those for the garnish). Cover and cook for another 10–15 minutes. Serve garnished with the rest of the blackberries and the sprig of lemon balm.

Chicken with Cajun Sauce

Sizzling fried chicken served in a tasty tomato sauce.

Serves 4

1 chicken, $3^1/_2$ pounds, cut into 8 pieces

$^3/_4$ cup all-purpose flour

1 cup buttermilk or milk

vegetable oil, for frying

salt and black pepper

chopped scallions, to garnish

For the sauce

$^2/_3$ cup crisco or vegetable oil

9 tablespoons all-purpose flour

2 onions, chopped

2–3 celery stalks, chopped

1 large green bell pepper, seeded
    and chopped

2 garlic cloves, finely chopped

1 cup puréed tomatoes

$1^7/_8$ cups red wine or homemade
    or canned chicken stock

$1^3/_4$ cups tomatoes, skinned
    and chopped

2 bay leaves

1 tablespoon brown sugar

1 teaspoon grated orange rind

$^1/_2$ teaspoon cayenne pepper

1 To make the sauce, heat the lard or oil in a large, heavy pan and stir in the flour. Cook over medium low heat, stirring constantly, for 15–20 minutes, or until the mixture has darkened to the color of hazelnut shells.

2 Add the chopped onions, celery, green pepper and garlic and cook, stirring, until the vegetables are softened.

3 Stir in the remaining sauce ingredients with salt and pepper to taste. Bring to a boil, then simmer for 1 hour, or until the sauce is rich and thick. Stir occasionally.

4 Meanwhile, prepare the chicken. Put the flour in a plastic bag and season with salt and pepper. Dip each piece of chicken in buttermilk, then dredge in the flour to coat lightly all over. Shake off excess flour. Set the chicken aside for 20 minutes to let the coating set before frying.

5 Heat the vegetable oil 1 inch deep in a large frying pan until it is very hot and starting to sizzle. Fry the chicken pieces, turning them once, for about 30 minutes or until deep golden brown all over and cooked through.

6 Drain the chicken pieces on paper towels. Add them to the sauce and sprinkle with chopped scallions.

Pot Roast Chicken with Sausage Stuffing

These casseroled chickens will be tender and succulent.

Serves 6

2 chickens, $2^1/_2$ pounds each

2 tablespoons vegetable oil

$1^1/_2$ cups homemade or canned chicken
   stock or half wine and half stock

1 bay leaf

For the stuffing

1 pound sausage

1 small onion, chopped

1–2 garlic cloves, finely chopped

1 teaspoon hot paprika

$^1/_2$ teaspoon dried chili
   (optional)

$^1/_2$ teaspoon dried thyme

$^1/_4$ teaspoon ground allspice

1 cup coarse fresh breadcrumbs

1 egg, beaten to mix

salt and black pepper

1 Preheat the oven to 350°F.

2 For the stuffing, put the sausage, onion and garlic in a frying pan and fry over medium heat until the sausage is lightly browned and crumbly, stirring and turning so it cooks evenly. Remove from the heat and mix in the remaining stuffing ingredients with salt and pepper to taste.

3 Divide the stuffing between the chickens, packing it into the body cavities (or, if preferred, stuff the neck end and bake the leftover stuffing in a separate dish). Truss the birds.

4 Heat the oil in a flameproof casserole just big enough to hold the chickens. Brown the birds all over.

5 Add the stock and bay leaf and season. Cover and bring to a boil, then transfer to the oven. Roast, covered, for $1^1/_4$ hours or until the birds are cooked (the juices will run clear).

6 Untruss the chickens and spoon the stuffing onto a serving platter. Arrange the birds and serve with the strained cooking liquid.

VARIATION

For Pot Roast Guinea Hens, use 2 guinea hens instead of chickens.

Rock Cornish Hens Waldorf

Sunday roast and stuffing, with a difference.

INGREDIENTS

Serves 6

6 Rock Cornish hens, about
   1^1/$_4$ pounds each

salt and black pepper

3–4 tablespoons butter or margarine
   melted

For the stuffing

2 tablespoons butter

1 onion, finely chopped

2^1/$_4$ cups cooked rice

2 celery stalks, finely chopped

2 red apples, cored and finely diced

^{1}/$_3$ cup walnuts, chopped

5 tablespoons cream sherry or apple juice

2 tablespoons lemon juice

1 Preheat the oven to 350°F. To make the stuffing, melt the butter in a small frying pan and fry the onion, stirring occasionally, until soft. Pour the onion and butter into a bowl and add the remaining stuffing ingredients. Season with salt and pepper and mix well.

2 Divide the stuffing among the birds, stuffing the body cavities. Truss the birds and arrange in a roasting pan. Sprinkle with salt and pepper and drizzle on the melted butter.

3 Roast for about 1^1/$_4$–1^1/$_2$ hours. Untruss before serving.

CARVING POULTRY

Carving a bird neatly for serving makes the presentation attractive. You will need a sharp long-bladed knife, or an electric knife, plus a long 2-pronged fork and a carving board with a groove around the border to catch the juices.

   Cut away any trussing string. For a stuffed bird, spoon the stuffing from the cavity into a serving dish. For easier carving, remove the wishbone.

   Insert the fork into one breast to hold the bird steady. Cut through the skin to the ball and socket joint on that side of the body, then slice through it to sever the leg from the body. Repeat on the other side.

1 Slice through the ball and socket joint in each leg to sever the thigh and drumstick. If carving turkey, slice the meat off the thigh and drumstick, parallel to the bone, turning to get even slices; leave chicken thighs and drumsticks whole.

2 To carve the breast of a turkey or chicken, cut ^{1}/$_4$-inch thick slices at an angle, slicing down on both sides of the breastbone. For smaller birds, remove the meat on each side of the breastbone in a single piece, then slice across.

Chicken Brunswick Stew

This is chicken stew with a spicy bite, warming and filling.

INGREDIENTS

Serves 6

4 pounds chicken, cut in
    serving pieces
paprika
2 tablespoons olive oil
2 tablespoons butter
2 cups chopped onions
1 cup chopped green or yellow
    bell peppers
2 cups chopped peeled fresh or canned
    plum tomatoes
1 cup white wine
2 cups chicken homemade or canned
    stock or water
1/4 cup chopped fresh parsley
1/2 teaspoon hot pepper sauce
1 tablespoon Worcestershire sauce
2 cups corn (fresh, frozen
    or canned)
1 cup lima beans (fresh or frozen)
3 tablespoons all-purpose flour
salt and black pepper
rolls, rice, or potatoes, for serving
    (optional)

1 Pat the chicken pieces dry, then sprinkle them lightly with salt and paprika.

2 In a large heavy saucepan, heat the olive oil with the butter over medium-high heat. Heat until the mixture is sizzling and just starting to change color.

3 Add the chicken pieces and fry until golden brown on all sides. Remove the chicken pieces with tongs and set aside.

4 Reduce the heat to low and add the chopped onions and peppers to the pan. Cook until softened, 8–10 minutes.

5 Raise the heat. Add the tomatoes and their juice, the wine, stock or water, parsley, and hot pepper and Worcestershire sauces. Stir and bring to a boil.

6 Return the fried chicken pieces to the pan, pushing them down in the sauce. Cover, reduce the heat, and simmer 30 minutes, stirring occasionally.

7 Add the corn and lima beans and mix well. Partly cover and cook 30 minutes more.

8 Tilt the pan and skim off as much of the surface fat as possible. In a small bowl, mix the flour with a little water to make a paste.

9 Gradually stir in about 3/4 cup of the hot sauce from the pan. Stir the flour mixture into the stew, and mix well to distribute it evenly and to thicken the stew. Cook 5–8 minutes more, stirring occasionally.

10 Check the seasoning. Serve the stew in shallow soup plates or large bowls.

Chicken with Sage, Prunes and Brandy

*This stir-fry has a very rich sauce
based on a good brandy – use the
best you can afford.*

INGREDIENTS

Serves 4

4 ounces prunes

3–3$^{1}/_{2}$ pounds boneless chicken
   breast

1$^{1}/_{4}$ cups cognac or brandy

1 tablespoon fresh sage, chopped

5 ounces smoked bacon, in one piece

4 tablespoons butter

24 baby onions, peeled and quartered

salt and black pepper

fresh sage sprigs, to garnish

1 Pit the prunes and cut them
into slivers. Remove the skin
from the chicken and cut the
breast into thin pieces.

2 Mix together the prunes,
chicken, cognac and chopped
sage in a non-metallic dish. Cover
and let marinate overnight.

3 Next day, strain the chicken
and prunes, reserving the
cognac marinade mixture, and pat
dry on paper towels.

4 Cut the smoked bacon into
dice and set aside. Heat a wok
or large frying pan and add half
the butter. When the butter has
melted, add the onions and stir-fry
for 4 minutes, until crisp and
golden. Then set aside.

5 Add the bacon to the wok and
stir-fry for 1 minute, until it
begins to release some fat. Add the
remaining butter and stir-fry the
chicken and prunes for 3–4
minutes, until crisp and golden.
Push the chicken mixture to one
side in the wok, add the cognac and
simmer until thickened. Stir the
chicken into the sauce, season well
with salt and pepper, and serve
garnished with sage.

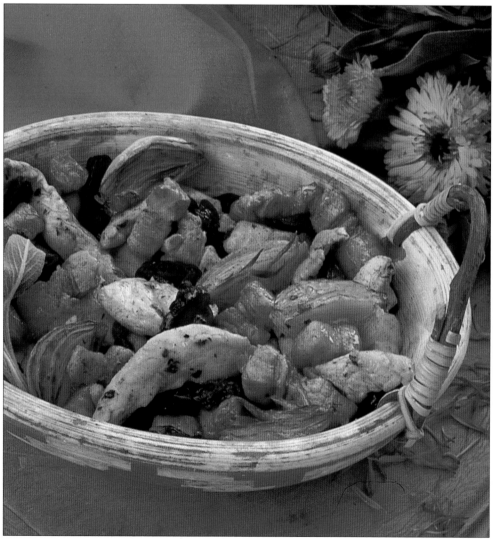

Pasta Sauce with Chicken and Tomato

*Perfect for a speedy supper – serve
this with a mixed bean salad.*

INGREDIENTS

Serves 4

1 tablespoon olive oil

1 onion, chopped

1 carrot, chopped

1 cup sun-dried tomatoes in olive oil

1 garlic clove, chopped

14-ounce can chopped tomatoes, drained

1 tablespoon tomato paste

$2/3$ cup homemade or canned
  chicken stock

3 cups pasta spirals (fusilli)

8 ounces chicken, diagonally sliced

salt and black pepper

sprigs fresh mint, to garnish

1 Heat the oil in a large frying
pan and fry the chopped onion
and carrot for 5 minutes, stirring
occasionally.

2 Chop the sun-dried tomatoes
and set aside.

3 Stir the garlic, canned tomatoes, tomato paste and stock
into the onions and carrots and
bring to a boil. Simmer for 10
minutes, stirring occasionally.

4 Cook the pasta in plenty of
water, following the instructions on the package.

5 Pour the sauce into a food
processor or blender and
process until smooth.

COOK'S TIP

Sun-dried tomatoes are sold
soaked in vegetable or olive oil in
jars. The olive oil-soaked
tomatoes have a superior flavor.
For extra flavor, fry the onion
and carrot in 1 tablespoon of the
oil from the tomatoes.

6 Return the sauce to the pan
and stir in the sun-dried tomatoes and chicken. Bring back to a
boil, then simmer for 10 minutes
until the chicken is cooked. Adjust
the seasoning.

7 Drain the pasta thoroughly and
toss it with the sauce. Serve
immediately, garnished with sprigs
of fresh mint.

Chicken with Sloe Gin and Juniper

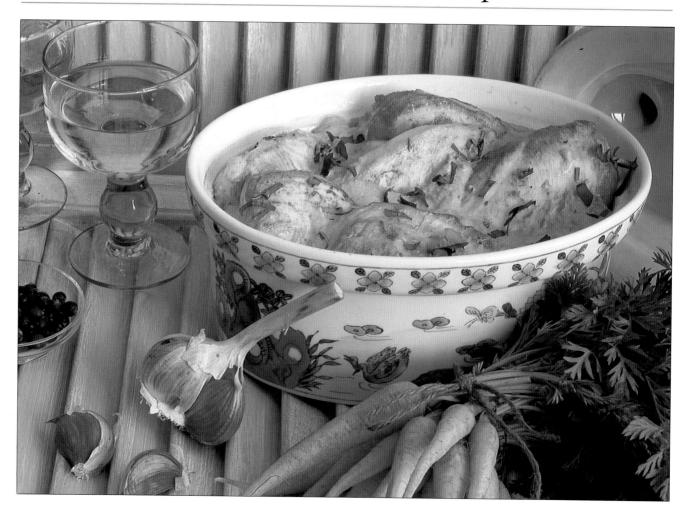

Juniper is used in the manufacture of gin, and the reinforcement of the flavor by using both sloe gin and juniper is delicious. Sloe gin is easy to make, but can also be bought ready-made.

INGREDIENTS

Serves 8

2 tablespoons butter

2 tablespoons sunflower oil

8 chicken breast fillets

12 ounces carrots, cooked

1 clove garlic, crushed

1 tablespoon finely chopped parsley

1/4 cup homemade or canned
chicken stock

1/4 cup red wine

1/4 cup sloe gin

1 teaspoon crushed juniper berries

salt and black pepper

chopped fresh basil, to garnish

1 Melt the butter with the oil in a frying pan, and fry the chicken until browned on all sides.

2 In a food processor or blender, combine all the remaining ingredients except the basil, and blend to a smooth paste. If the mixture seems too thick, add a little more red wine or water.

3 Put the chicken fillets in a clean pan, pour the sauce on top and cook over medium heat until the chicken is cooked through – about 15 minutes. Adjust the seasoning and serve garnished with chopped fresh basil.

Chicken with Figs and Mint

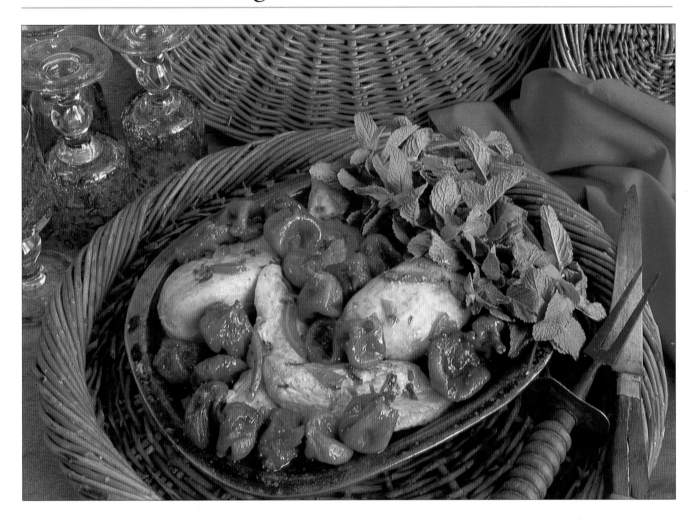

Refreshing mint and orange flavors go well with chicken.

INGREDIENTS

Serves 4

3 1/3 cups dried figs

1/2 bottle sweet, fruity white wine

4 boneless chicken breasts, about
    6–8 ounces each

1 tablespoon butter

2 tablespoons dark orange marmalade

10 mint leaves, finely chopped, plus a few
    more to garnish

juice of 1/2 lemon

salt and black pepper

1 Place the figs in a pan with the wine and bring to a boil, then simmer very gently for about 1 hour. Let cool and refrigerate overnight.

2 Fry the chicken breasts in the butter until they are cooked. Remove and keep warm. Drain any fat from the pan and pour in the juice from the figs. Boil and reduce to about 2/3 cup.

3 Add the marmalade, chopped mint leaves and lemon juice, and simmer for a few minutes. Season to taste. When the sauce is thick and shiny, pour it on the chicken, garnish with the figs and mint leaves and serve.

Chicken with Sauce Piquant

Sauce Piquant goes with everything that runs, flies or swims in Louisiana – you will even find Alligator with Sauce Piquant on menus. It is based on the brown Cajun roux, and chili peppers give it heat; vary the number you use.

INGREDIENTS

Serves 4

4 chicken legs or 2 legs and 2 breasts

^{1}/$_3$ cup cooking oil

^{1}/$_2$ cup all-purpose flour

1 medium onion, chopped

2 celery stalks, sliced

1 green bell pepper, seeded and diced

2 garlic cloves, crushed

1 bay leaf

^{1}/$_2$ teaspoon dried thyme

^{1}/$_2$ teaspoon dried oregano

1–2 red chili peppers, seeded and finely
    chopped

14-ounce can tomatoes, chopped, with
    their juice

1^1/$_4$ cups homemade or canned
    chicken stock

salt and black pepper

watercress to garnish

boiled potatoes to serve

1 Halve the chicken legs through the joint, or the breasts across the middle, to make 8 pieces.

2 In a heavy frying pan, fry the chicken pieces in the oil until brown on all sides, setting them aside as they are done.

3 Strain the oil from the pan into a heavy flameproof casserole. Heat it and stir in the flour. Stir constantly over a low heat until the roux is the color of peanut butter.

4 As soon as the roux reaches the right stage, add the onion, celery and pepper and stir over the heat for 2–3 minutes.

5 Add the garlic, bay leaf, thyme, oregano and chili pepper(s). Stir for 1 minute, then turn down the heat and stir in the tomatoes with their juice.

6 Return the casserole to the heat and gradually stir in the stock. Add the chicken pieces, cover and let simmer for 45 minutes, or until the chicken is tender.

7 If there is too much sauce or if it looks too runny, remove the lid for the last 10–15 minutes of the cooking time and turn up the heat a little.

8 Check the seasoning and serve, garnished with watercress and accompanied by boiled potatoes.

COOK'S TIP

If you prefer to err on the side of caution with chili heat, use just 1 chili pepper and heat up the seasoning at the end with a dash or two of Tabasco sauce. The oil in chili peppers clings to your skin and could hurt if you then rub your eyes. Scrape out the seeds under cold running water and wash your hands after handling chilies.

Stuffed Chicken Wings

These tasty stuffed wings can be served hot or cold at a buffet. They can be prepared and frozen in advance.

Makes 12

12 large chicken wings

For the filling

1 teaspoon cornstarch

$^{1}/_{4}$ teaspoon salt

$^{1}/_{2}$ teaspoon fresh thyme

pinch of black pepper

For the coating

3 cups dried breadcrumbs

2 tablespoons sesame seeds

2 eggs, beaten

oil, for deep-frying

1 Remove the wing tips and discard or use them for making stock. Skin the second joint sections, removing the two small bones, and reserve the meat for the filling.

2 Grind the reserved meat and mix with the filling ingredients.

3 Holding the large end of the bone on the third section of the wing and using a sharp knife, cut the skin and flesh away from the bone, scraping down and pulling the meat over the small end to form a pocket. Repeat this process with the remaining wing sections.

4 Fill the tiny pockets with the filling. Mix the dried bread-crumbs and the sesame seeds together. Place the breadcrumb mixture and the beaten egg in separate dishes.

5 Brush the meat with beaten egg and roll in breadcrumbs to cover. Chill and repeat to make a second layer, forming a thick coating. Chill until ready to fry.

6 Preheat the oven to 350°F. Heat 2 inches of oil in a heavy pan until hot but not smoking, or the breadcrumbs will burn. Gently fry two or three wings at a time until golden brown, remove and drain on paper towels. Complete the cooking in the preheated oven for 15–20 minutes, until tender.

Penne with Chicken and Ham Sauce

A meal in itself, this colorful pasta sauce is perfect for lunch or dinner.

INGREDIENTS

Serves 4

3 cups penne
2 tablespoons butter
1 onion, chopped
1 garlic clove, chopped
1 bay leaf
2 cups dry white wine
$2/3$ cup crème fraîche
$1^1/_2$ cups cooked chicken, skinned,
   boned and diced
$2/3$ cup cooked lean ham, diced
1 cup grated Gouda cheese
1 tablespoon chopped fresh mint
salt and black pepper
finely shredded fresh mint, to garnish

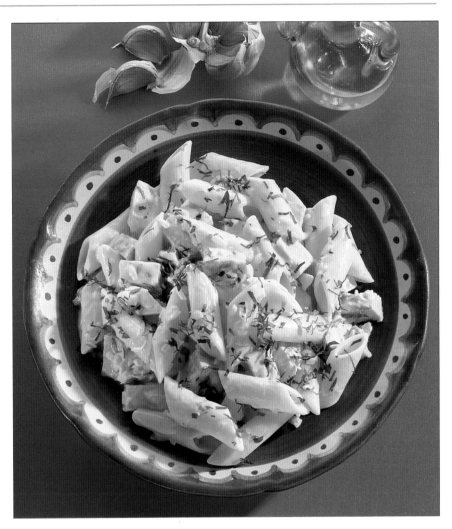

1 Cook the pasta in plenty of water, following the instructions on the package.

2 Heat the butter in a large frying pan and fry the onion for 10 minutes, until softened.

COOK'S TIP
∾
Crème fraîche is a richer, full-fat French cream with a slightly acidic taste. If you can't find any, substitute sour cream.

3 Add the garlic, bay leaf and wine and bring to a boil. Boil rapidly until reduced by half. Remove the bay leaf, then stir in the crème fraîche and bring back to a boil.

4 Add the chicken, ham and cheese and simmer for 5 minutes, stirring occasionally, until heated through.

5 Add the mint and seasoning. Drain the pasta and turn it into a large serving bowl. Toss with the sauce immediately and garnish with shredded mint.

Tagliatelle with Chicken and Herb Sauce

This wine-flavored sauce is best served with green salad.

INGREDIENTS

Serves 4

2 tablespoons olive oil

1 red onion, cut into wedges

12 ounces tagliatelle

1 garlic clove, chopped

$2^1/_2$ cups chicken, diced

$1^1/_4$ cups dry vermouth

3 tablespoons chopped fresh mixed herbs

$^2/_3$ cup ricotta or farmer's cheese

salt and black pepper

shredded fresh mint, to garnish

1 Heat the oil in a large frying pan and fry the onion for 10 minutes until softened, and the layers begin to separate.

2 Cook the pasta in plenty of water, following the instructions on the package.

COOK'S TIP

If you don't want to use vermouth, use dry white wine instead. Orvieto and frascati are two Italian wines that are ideal to use in this sauce.

3 Add the garlic and chicken to the frying pan and fry for 10 minutes, stirring occasionally, until the chicken is browned all over and cooked through.

4 Pour in the vermouth, bring to a boil and boil rapidly until reduced by about half.

5 Stir in the herbs, cheese and seasoning and heat through gently, but do not boil.

6 Drain the pasta thoroughly and toss it with the sauce to coat. Serve immediately, garnished with shredded fresh mint.

Risotto

An Italian dish made with short grain arborio rice, which gives a creamy consistency to this easy one-pan recipe.

INGREDIENTS

Serves 4

1 tablespoon oil

1 cup arborio rice

1 onion, chopped

2 cups ground chicken

2¹/₂ cups homemade or canned
    chicken stock

1 red bell pepper, seeded and chopped

1 yellow bell pepper, seeded and chopped

³/₄ cup frozen green beans

1¹/₂ cups Crimini
    mushrooms, sliced

1 tablespoon chopped fresh parsley

salt and black pepper

fresh parsley, to garnish

3 Pour in the stock and bring to a boil.

4 Stir in the peppers and reduce the heat. Cook for 10 minutes.

5 Add the green beans and mushrooms and cook for another 10 minutes.

6 Stir in the fresh parsley and season well to taste. Cook for 10 minutes, or until the liquid has been absorbed. Serve garnished with fresh parsley.

1 Heat the oil in a large frying pan. Add the rice and cook for 2 minutes, until transparent.

2 Add the onion and ground chicken. Cook for 5 minutes, stirring occasionally.

SALADS
& BARBECUES

Chicken Pitas with Red Coleslaw

Pitas are convenient for simple snacks and packed lunches and it's easy to pack them with lots of fresh, healthy ingredients.

INGREDIENTS

Serves 4

1/4 red cabbage

1 small red onion, finely sliced

2 radishes, thinly sliced

1 red apple, peeled, cored and grated

1 tablespoon lemon juice

3 tablespoons ricotta cheese

1 cooked chicken breast without skin, about 6 ounces

4 large or 8 small pitas

salt and black pepper

chopped fresh parsley, to garnish

1 Remove the tough central spine from the cabbage leaves, then finely shred the leaves using a large sharp knife. Place the shredded cabbage in a bowl and stir in the onion, radishes, apple and lemon juice.

2 Stir the ricotta cheese into the shredded cabbage mixture and season well with salt and pepper. Thinly slice the cooked chicken breast and stir into the cabbage mixture until well coated with ricotta.

3 Sprinkle the pitas with a little water, warm them in a hot oven, then split them along one edge using a round-bladed knife. Divide the filling equally among the pitas, then garnish with chopped fresh parsley.

COOK'S TIP

If the filled pitas need to be made more than an hour in advance, line the pita breads with crisp lettuce leaves before adding the filling.

Caribbean Chicken Kebabs

These kebabs have a rich, sunny Caribbean flavor, and the marinade keeps them moist without the need for oil. Serve with a colorful salad and rice.

INGREDIENTS

Serves 4

1¹/₄ pounds chicken breasts, boned and
    skinned

finely grated rind of 1 lime

2 tablespoons lime juice

1 tablespoon rum or sherry

1 tablespoon light brown sugar

1 teaspoon ground cinnamon

2 mangoes, peeled and cubed

rice and salad, to serve

1 Cut the chicken breasts into bite-size chunks and place in a bowl with the grated lime rind and juice, rum or sherry, sugar and cinnamon. Toss well, cover and marinate for 1 hour.

COOK'S TIP

The rum or sherry adds a terrific rich flavor, but it is optional so can be omitted if you prefer to make the dish more economical.

2 Save the juices, and thread the chicken onto four wooden skewers, alternating with the mango cubes.

3 Cook the kebabs under a hot broiler or barbecue for 8–10 minutes, turning occasionally and basting with the reserved juices, until the chicken is tender and golden brown. Serve at once with rice and salad.

Grilled Chicken

The flavor of this dish, known in Indonesia as Ayam Bakur, *will be more intense if the chicken is marinated overnight. It is an ideal recipe for a party, because the final broiling, barbecuing or baking can be done at the last minute.*

INGREDIENTS

Serves 4

1 chicken, 3–3¹/₂ pounds

4 garlic cloves, crushed

2 lemon grass stems, lower 2 inches sliced

1 teaspoon ground turmeric

2 cups water

3–4 bay leaves

3 tablespoons each dark and light soy sauce

¹/₄ cup butter or margarine

salt

boiled rice, to serve

1 Cut the chicken into 4 or 8 portions. Slash the fleshy part of each portion twice and set aside.

2 Grind the garlic, sliced lemon grass, turmeric and salt together into a paste in a food processor or with a mortar and pestle. Rub the paste into the chicken pieces and leave for at least 30 minutes. Wear rubber gloves for this, as the turmeric will stain; or wash your hands immediately after mixing, if you prefer.

3 Transfer the chicken to a wok and pour in the water. Add the bay leaves and bring to a boil. Cover and cook gently for 30 minutes, adding a little more water, if necessary, and stirring occasionally.

4 Just before serving, add the two soy sauces to the pan together with the butter or margarine.

5 Cook until the chicken is well-coated and the sauce has almost been absorbed. Transfer the chicken to a preheated broiler or barbecue, or an oven preheated to 400°F, to complete the cooking. Cook for another 10–15 minutes, turning the pieces often so they become golden brown all over. Take care not to let them burn. Baste with remaining sauce during cooking. Serve with boiled rice.

Dijon Chicken Salad

An attractive dish to serve for lunch with herb and garlic bread.

INGREDIENTS

Serves 4

4 chicken breasts, boned and skinned

mixed salad leaves, such as frisée and
    oakleaf lettuce or radicchio, to serve

For the marinade

2 tablespoons Dijon mustard

3 garlic cloves, crushed

1 tablespoon grated onion

4 tablespoons white wine

For the mustard dressing

2 tablespoons tarragon vinegar

1 teaspoon Dijon mustard

1 teaspoon honey

6 tablespoons olive oil

salt and black pepper

1 Mix all the marinade ingredients in a shallow glass or ceramic dish that is large enough to hold the chicken in a single layer.

2 Turn the chicken over in the marinade to coat completely, cover with plastic wrap and chill in the fridge overnight.

3 Preheat the oven to 375°F. Transfer the chicken and the marinade to an ovenproof dish, cover with foil and bake for about 35 minutes, or until tender. Set aside to cool.

4 Put all the mustard dressing ingredients into a screw-top jar, shake vigorously to emulsify, and adjust the seasoning. (This can be made several days in advance and stored in the fridge.)

5 Slice the chicken thinly, fan out the slices and arrange on a serving dish with the salad leaves.

6 Spoon on some of the mustard dressing and serve.

Lemon Chicken with Guacamole Sauce

The avocado sauce makes an unusual accompaniment to the grilled chicken.

Serves 4

juice of 2 lemons

3 tablespoons olive oil

2 garlic cloves, crushed

4 chicken breast halves, about
    7 ounces each

2 beefsteak tomatoes, cored and halved

salt and black pepper

chopped fresh cilantro, to garnish

For the sauce

1 ripe avocado

$^1/_4$ cup sour cream

3 tablespoons fresh lemon juice

$^1/_2$ teaspoon salt

$^1/_4$ cup water

1 Combine the lemon juice, oil, garlic, $^1/_2$ teaspoon salt, and a little pepper in a bowl. Stir to mix.

2 Arrange the chicken breasts in one layer, in a shallow glass or ceramic dish. Pour on the lemon mixture and turn to coat evenly. Cover and let stand at least 1 hour at room temperature, or refrigerate overnight.

3 For the sauce, cut the avocado in half, remove the pit, and scrape the flesh into a food processor or blender.

4 Add the sour cream, lemon juice, and salt and process until smooth. Add the water and process just to blend. If necessary, add more water to thin the sauce. Transfer to a bowl, taste and adjust the seasoning, if necessary. Set aside.

5 Preheat the broiler. Also heat a ridged stovetop grill pan. Remove the chicken from the marinade and pat dry.

6 When the grill pan is hot, add the chicken breasts and cook, turning often, until they are cooked through, about 10 minutes.

7 Meanwhile, arrange the tomato halves, cut sides up, on a baking sheet and season lightly with salt and pepper. Broil until hot and bubbling, about 5 minutes.

8 To serve, place a chicken breast, tomato half, and a dollop of avocado sauce on each plate. Sprinkle with cilantro and serve.

VARIATION

To barbecue the chicken, light the barbecue grill, and when the coals are glowing red and covered with gray ash, spread them in a single layer. Set an oiled grill rack about 5 inches above the coals and cook the chicken breasts until lightly charred and cooked through, about 15–20 minutes. Use extra olive oil for basting.

Chicken Liver Kebabs

These may be barbecued outdoors and served with salads and baked potatoes, or broiled indoors and served with rice and broccoli.

INGREDIENTS

Serves 4

4 ounces lean bacon strips

12 ounces chicken livers

12 large pitted prunes

12 cherry tomatoes

8 button mushrooms

2 tablespoons olive oil

1 Cut each strip of bacon into two pieces, wrap a piece around each chicken liver and secure in place with wooden toothpicks.

2 Wrap the pitted prunes around the cherry tomatoes.

3 Thread the bacon-wrapped livers onto metal skewers with the tomatoes, prunes and mushrooms. Brush with oil. Cover the tomatoes and prunes with a strip of foil to protect them while broiling or barbecuing. Cook for 5 minutes on each side.

4 Remove the toothpicks and serve the kebabs immediately.

Citrus Kebabs

Serve on a bed of lettuce leaves and garnish with fresh mint and orange and lemon slices.

Serves 4

4 chicken breasts, skinned and boned

fresh mint sprigs, to garnish

orange, lemon or lime slices, to garnish
(optional)

For the marinade

finely grated rind and juice of $^1/_2$ orange

finely grated rind and juice of $^1/_2$ small
lemon or lime

2 tablespoons olive oil

2 tablespoons honey

2 tablespoons chopped fresh mint

$^1/_4$ teaspoon ground cumin

salt and black pepper

1 Cut the chicken breasts into
1-inch cubes.

2 Mix the marinade ingredients
together in a glass or ceramic
bowl, add the chicken cubes and
marinate for at least 2 hours.

3 Thread the chicken pieces onto
skewers and broil or barbecue
over low coals for 15 minutes,
basting with the marinade and
turning frequently. Serve garnished
with extra mint and citrus slices, if
desired.

Chicken Satay

Marinate the chicken in the satay sauce overnight to allow the flavors to penetrate it. Soak wooden skewers in water overnight to prevent them from burning while cooking.

INGREDIENTS

Serves 4

4 chicken breasts

lemon slices, to garnish

lettuce leaves, to serve

scallions, to serve

For the satay

$^1/_2$ cup crunchy peanut butter

1 small onion, chopped

1 garlic clove, crushed

2 tablespoons chutney

4 tablespoons olive oil

1 teaspoon light soy sauce

2 tablespoons lemon juice

$^1/_4$ teaspoon ground chilies or
   cayenne pepper

1 Put all the satay ingredients into a food processor or blender and process until smooth. Spoon into a large dish.

2 Remove all bone and skin from the chicken and cut into 1-inch cubes. Add to the satay mixture and stir to coat the chicken pieces. Cover with plastic wrap and chill for at least 4 hours or, better still, overnight.

3 Preheat the broiler or grill. Thread the chicken pieces onto the wooden skewers.

4 Cook for 10 minutes, brushing occasionally with the satay sauce. Serve on a bed of lettuce and scallions, and garnish with lemon slices.

Chicken and Pasta Salad

*This is a delicious way to use up
leftover cooked chicken.*

INGREDIENTS

Serves 4

2 cups tri-colored pasta twists

2 tablespoons pesto sauce

1 tablespoon olive oil

1 beefsteak tomato

12 pitted black olives

$1^1/_2$ cups cooked green beans

3 cups cooked chicken, cubed

salt and black pepper

fresh basil, to garnish

1 Cook the pasta in plenty of boiling, salted water until al dente (about 12 minutes or as directed on the package).

2 Drain the pasta and rinse in plenty of cold running water. Put into a bowl and stir in the pesto sauce and olive oil.

3 Peel the tomato, first by placing in boiling water for about 10 seconds and then into cold water, to loosen the skin.

4 Cut the tomato into small cubes and add to the pasta with the olives, seasoning and green beans cut into $1^1/_2$-inch lengths. Add the cubed chicken. Toss gently together and transfer to a serving platter. Garnish with fresh basil.

Barbecued Jerk Chicken

Jerk refers to the blend of herb and spice seasoning rubbed into meat before it is roasted over charcoal sprinkled with pimiento berries. In Jamaica, jerk seasoning was originally used only for pork, but jerked chicken is equally good.

INGREDIENTS

Serves 4

8 chicken pieces

For the marinade

1 teaspoon ground allspice
1 teaspoon ground cinnamon
1 teaspoon dried thyme
$1/4$ teaspoon freshly grated nutmeg
2 teaspoons raw sugar
2 garlic cloves, crushed
1 tablespoon finely chopped onion
1 tablespoon chopped scallion
1 tablespoon vinegar
2 tablespoons peanut oil
1 tablespoon lime juice
1 hot chili pepper, chopped
salt and black pepper
lettuce leaves, to serve

1 Combine all the marinade ingredients in a small bowl. Using a fork, mash them together well to form a thick paste.

2 Lay the chicken pieces on a plate or board and make several lengthwise slits in the flesh. Rub the seasoning all over the chicken and into the slits.

3 Place the chicken pieces in a dish, cover with plastic wrap and marinate overnight in the fridge. Shake off any excess seasoning from the chicken. Brush with oil and place either on a baking sheet or a barbecue grill, if barbecuing.

4 Cook under a preheated broiler for 45 minutes, turning often. Or, if barbecuing, light the coals and when ready, cook over the coals for 30 minutes, turning often. Serve hot with lettuce leaves.

COOK'S TIP

The flavor is best if you marinate the chicken overnight.

Grilled Butterflied Rock Cornish Hens

Grilled Rock Cornish hens with an onion and herb dressing.

Serves 4

4 Rock Cornish hens, about 1 pound each, butterflied

olive oil

salt and black pepper

For the onion and herb sauce

2 tablespoons dry sherry

2 tablespoons lemon juice

2 tablespoons olive oil

2 ounces scallions, chopped

1 garlic clove, finely chopped

4 tablespoons chopped mixed fresh herbs such as tarragon, parsley, thyme, marjoram, and lemon balm

1 Preheat the broiler to high, or prepare a charcoal grill.

2 Season the butterflied birds, then brush them with a little olive oil. Set them on the rack in the broiler pan about 4 inches from the heat, or on the barbecue grill 6 inches above the coals.

3 Cook for 20–25 minutes, or until tender. Turn and brush with more oil halfway through the cooking time.

4 Meanwhile, to make the sauce, whisk together the sherry, lemon juice, olive oil, scallions and garlic. Season with salt and pepper.

5 When the birds are done, transfer them to a deep serving platter. Whisk the herbs into the sauce, then spoon it on the birds. Cover tightly with another platter or with foil and let rest for 15 minutes before serving.

Chinese-style Chicken Salad

Shredded chicken is served with a tasty peanut sauce.

INGREDIENTS

Serves 4

4 boneless chicken breasts, about
   6 ounces each

4 tablespoons dark soy sauce

pinch of Chinese five-spice powder

a good squeeze of lemon juice

$1/2$ cucumber, peeled and cut into
   matchsticks

1 teaspoon salt

3 tablespoons sunflower oil

2 tablespoons sesame oil

1 tablespoon sesame seeds

2 tablespoons dry sherry

2 carrots, cut into matchsticks

8 scallions, shredded

$1/2$ cup beansprouts

For the sauce

4 tablespoons crunchy peanut butter

2 teaspoons lemon juice

2 teaspoons sesame oil

$1/4$ teaspoon ground hot chilies

1 scallion, finely chopped

1 Put the chicken pieces into a
large pan and just cover with
water. Add 1 tablespoon of the soy
sauce, the Chinese five-spice
powder and lemon juice, cover and
bring to a boil, then simmer for
about 20 minutes.

2 Place the cucumber
matchsticks in a colander,
sprinkle with the salt and cover
with a weighted plate on top.
Let drain for 30 minutes.

3 Heat the oils in a large frying
pan or wok. Add the sesame
seeds, fry for 30 seconds and then
stir in the remaining soy sauce
and the sherry. Add the carrots
and stir-fry for 2–3 minutes.
Remove and reserve.

4 Remove the chicken from the
pan and let stand until cool
enough to handle. Discard the
skins and bash the chicken lightly
with a rolling pin to loosen the
fibers. Slice in strips and reserve.

5 Rinse the cucumber well, pat
dry with paper towels and
place in a bowl. Add the scallions,
beansprouts, cooked carrots, pan
juices and shredded chicken, and
mix together. Transfer to a shallow
dish. Cover and chill for about
1 hour, turning the mixture in the
juices once or twice.

6 To make the sauce, cream the
peanut butter with the lemon
juice, sesame oil and ground
chilies, adding a little hot water to
form a paste, then stir in the
scallion. Arrange the chicken
mixture on a serving dish and
serve with the peanut sauce.

Fusilli with Chicken, Tomatoes and Broccoli

This is a really hearty main-course salad for a hungry family.

INGREDIENTS

Serves 4

1¹/₂ pounds ripe but firm plum tomatoes, quartered

6 tablespoons olive oil

1 teaspoon dried oregano

salt and black pepper

12 ounces broccoli florets

1 small onion, sliced

1 teaspoon dried thyme

1 pound chicken breasts, boned, skinned and cubed

3 garlic cloves, crushed

1 tablespoon fresh lemon juice

1 pound fusilli

1 Preheat the oven to 400°F.

2 Place the tomatoes in a baking dish. Add 1 tablespoon of the oil, the oregano, and ¹/₂ teaspoon salt and stir to blend.

3 Bake until the tomatoes are just browned, about 30–40 minutes; do not stir.

4 Meanwhile, bring a large pan of salted water to a boil. Add the broccoli and cook until just tender, about 5 minutes. Drain and set aside. (Alternatively, steam the broccoli until tender.)

5 Heat 2 tablespoons of the oil in a large nonstick frying pan. Add the onion, thyme, chicken cubes and ¹/₂ teaspoon salt. Cook over high heat, stirring until the meat is cooked and beginning to brown, 5–7 minutes. Add the garlic and cook 1 minute more, stirring.

6 Remove from the heat. Stir in the lemon juice and season with pepper. Keep warm until the pasta is cooked.

7 Bring another large pan of salted water to a boil. Add the fusilli and cook until just tender (check the instructions on the package for timing). Drain and place in a large bowl. Toss with the remaining oil.

8 Add the broccoli to the chicken mixture. Add to the fusilli. Add the tomatoes and stir gently to blend. Serve immediately.

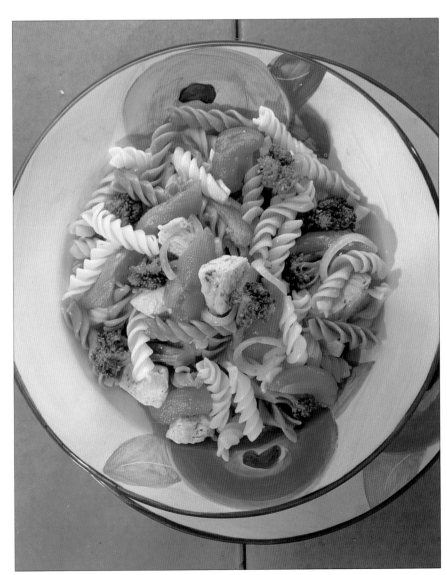

Swiss Cheese, Chicken and Tongue Salad

The rich sweet flavors of this salad marry well with the peppery watercress. A minted lemon dressing freshens the overall effect. Serve with new potatoes.

INGREDIENTS

Serves 4

2 free-range chicken breasts, skinned and boned

$1/2$ chicken bouillon cube

8 ounces sliced beef tongue or ham, $1/4$ inch thick

8 ounces Gruyère cheese

1 red leaf lettuce

1 Boston or curly endive lettuce

1 bunch watercress

2 green apples, cored and sliced

3 stalks celery, sliced

4 tablespoons sesame seeds, toasted

salt, black pepper and nutmeg

Dressing

5 tablespoons peanut or sunflower oil

1 teaspoon sesame oil

3 tablespoons lemon juice

2 teaspoons chopped fresh mint

3 drops Tabasco sauce

1 Place the chicken breasts in a shallow saucepan, cover with $1^{1}/4$ cups water, add the $1/2$ bouillon cube and bring to a boil. Put the lid on the pan and simmer for 15 minutes. Drain, reserving the stock for another occasion, then cool the chicken under cold running water.

2 To make the dressing, measure the two oils, lemon juice, mint and Tabasco sauce into a screw-top jar and shake. Cut the chicken, tongue and Gruyère cheese into fine strips. Moisten with a little dressing and set aside.

3 Combine the salad leaves with the apple and celery, and dress. Distribute among 4 large plates. Pile the chicken, tongue and cheese in the center, sprinkle with toasted sesame seeds, season with salt, pepper and freshly grated nutmeg and serve.

Chicken Liver, Bacon and Tomato Salad

Warm salads are especially welcome during the autumn months when the evenings are growing shorter and cooler. Try this rich salad with sweet spinach and bitter leaves of frisée lettuce.

INGREDIENTS

Serves 4

8 ounces young spinach, stems removed

1 frisée lettuce or curly endive

7 tablespoons peanut or sunflower oil

6 ounces rindless unsmoked bacon, cut into strips

3 ounces day-old bread, crusts removed and cut into short fingers

1 pound chicken livers

4 ounces cherry tomatoes

salt and black pepper

1 Place the salad leaves in a salad bowl. Heat 4 tablespoons of the oil in a large frying pan. Add the bacon and cook for 3–4 minutes, or until crisp and brown. Remove the bacon with a slotted spoon and drain on paper towels.

2 To make the croutons, fry the bread in the bacon-flavored oil, tossing until crisp and golden. Drain on paper towels.

3 Heat the remaining 3 tablespoons oil in the frying pan, add the chicken livers and fry briskly for 2–3 minutes. Pour over the salad leaves, and add the bacon, croutons and tomatoes. Season, toss and serve.

Wild Rice and Chicken Salad

Once you have cooked the wild rice, this is a very simple salad to make.

INGREDIENTS

Serves 4

1 cup (dry-weight) wild rice, boiled or
    steamed

2 stalks celery, thinly sliced

2 ounces scallions, chopped

1¹/₂ cups small button mushrooms,
    quartered

1 pound cooked chicken breast, diced

¹/₂ cup vinaigrette dressing

1 teaspoon fresh thyme leaves

2 pears, peeled, halved and cored

¹/₄ cup walnut pieces, toasted

1 Combine cooled cooked wild rice with the celery, scallions, mushrooms and chicken in a bowl.

2 Add the dressing and thyme; toss well together.

3 Thinly slice the pear halves lengthwise without cutting through the stem end and spread the slices into a fan. Divide the salad among 4 plates. Garnish each with a fanned pear half and walnuts.

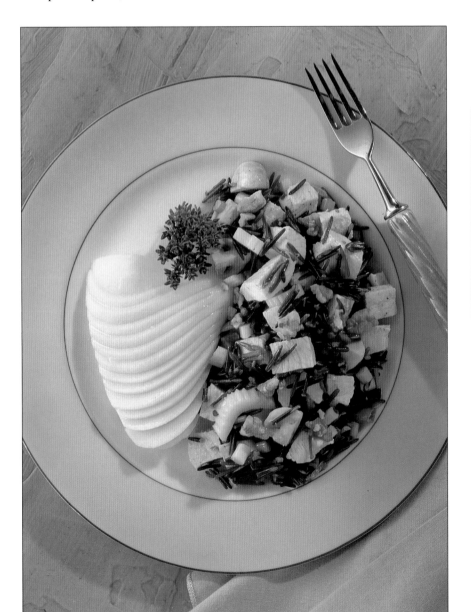

COOKING WILD RICE

To boil: Add the rice to a large pot of boiling salted water (about four parts water to each one of rice). Bring back to a gentle boil and cook for 45–50 minutes, or until the rice is tender but still firm and has begun to split open. Drain well.

To steam: Put the rice in a saucepan with the measured quantity of salted water. Bring to a boil, cover and steam over very low heat for 45–50 minutes, or until tender. Cook uncovered for the last 5 minutes to evaporate excess water.

Warm Chicken Liver Salad

Although warm salads may seem fussy or trendy, there are times when they are just right. Serve this delicious combination as either a first course or a light meal, with bread to dip into the dressing.

INGREDIENTS

Serves 4

4 ounces each fresh young spinach,
  arugula and red leaf lettuce

2 pink grapefruit

6 tablespoons sunflower oil

2 teaspoons sesame oil

2 teaspoons soy sauce

8 ounces chicken livers, chopped

salt and black pepper

1 Wash, dry and tear up all the leaves. Mix them well in a large salad bowl.

2 Carefully cut away all the peel and white pith from the grapefruit, then segment them, saving the juice. Add the grapefruit to the salad leaves.

3 To make the dressing, combine 4 tablespoons of the sunflower oil with the sesame oil, soy sauce, seasoning and grapefruit juice to taste.

4 Heat the rest of the sunflower oil in a small pan and cook the livers, stirring gently, until firm and lightly browned.

5 Pour the chicken livers and dressing over the salad and serve at once.

COOK'S TIP

Chicken or turkey livers are ideal for this recipe, and there's no need to leave them to defrost completely before cooking.

Orange Chicken Salad

A refreshing and very delicately flavored rice salad.

INGREDIENTS

Serves 4

3 large seedless oranges

1 cup long-grain rice

2 cups water

3/4 cup vinaigrette dressing, made with
    red wine vinegar and a mixture of olive
    and vegetable oils

2 teaspoons Dijon mustard

1/2 teaspoon sugar

1 pound cooked chicken, diced

3 tablespoons chopped chives

1/2 cup roasted cashews

salt and black pepper

cucumber slices, to garnish

1 Thinly peel 1 orange, taking only the colored part of the rind and leaving the white pith.

2 Combine the orange rind, rice and water in a saucepan. Add a pinch of salt. Bring to a boil, then cover and simmer over very low heat for 15–18 minutes, or until the rice is tender and all the water has been absorbed.

3 Peel the remaining oranges and cut out the segments, reserving the juice. Add the orange juice to the vinaigrette dressing. Add the mustard and sugar and whisk to combine well. Taste and add more salt and pepper if needed.

4 When the rice is cooked, remove it from the heat and cool slightly, uncovered. Discard the orange rind.

5 Turn the rice into a bowl and add half of the dressing. Toss well and cool completely.

6 Add the chicken, chives, cashews and orange segments to the rice with the remaining dressing. Toss gently. Serve at room temperature, garnished with cucumber.

Making Vinaigrette Dressing

A good vinaigrette can do more than dress a salad. It can also be used to baste meat, poultry, seafood or vegetables during cooking and it can be used as a flavoring and tenderizing marinade. The basic mixture of oil, vinegar and seasoning lends itself to many variations.

Vinaigrette dressing will keep in the fridge, in a tightly sealed container, for several weeks. Add flavorings, particularly fresh herbs, just before using.

INGREDIENTS

Makes just over 3/4 cup

3 tablespoons wine vinegar

salt and pepper

2/3 cup vegetable or olive oil

1 Put the vinegar, salt and pepper in a bowl and whisk to dissolve the salt. Gradually add the oil, stirring with the whisk. Taste and adjust seasoning.

Grilled Chicken Salad with Lavender

Lavender may seem like an odd salad ingredient, but its delightful scent has a natural affinity with sweet garlic, orange and other wild herbs. A serving of polenta makes this salad both filling and delicious.

INGREDIENTS

Serves 4

4 chicken breasts, boned

3³/4 cups homemade or canned
 chicken stock

1 cup fine polenta

4 tablespoons butter

1 pound young spinach

6 ounces lamb's lettuce or other very
 young lettuce

8 sprigs fresh lavender

8 small tomatoes, halved

salt and black pepper

Lavender Marinade

6 fresh lavender flowers

2 teaspoons finely grated orange rind

2 cloves garlic, crushed

2 teaspoons honey

salt

2 tablespoons olive oil

2 teaspoons chopped fresh thyme

2 teaspoons chopped fresh marjoram

1 To make the marinade, strip the lavender flowers from the stems and combine with the orange rind, garlic, honey and salt. Add the olive oil and herbs. Slash the chicken deeply, spread the mixture over the chicken and marinate in a cool place for at least 20 minutes.

2 To cook the polenta, bring the chicken stock to a boil in a heavy saucepan. Add the polenta in a steady stream, stirring all the time until thick: this will take 2–3 minutes. Turn the cooked polenta out onto a 1-inch-deep buttered tray and allow to cool.

3 Heat the broiler to medium. (If using a barbecue, let the embers settle to a steady glow.) Grill the chicken for about 15 minutes, turning once.

4 Cut the polenta into 1-inch cubes with a wet knife. Heat the butter in a large frying pan and fry the polenta until golden.

5 Wash the salad leaves and spin dry, then divide among 4 large plates. Slice each chicken breast and lay over the salad. Place the polenta among the salad, garnish with sprigs of lavender and tomatoes, season and serve.

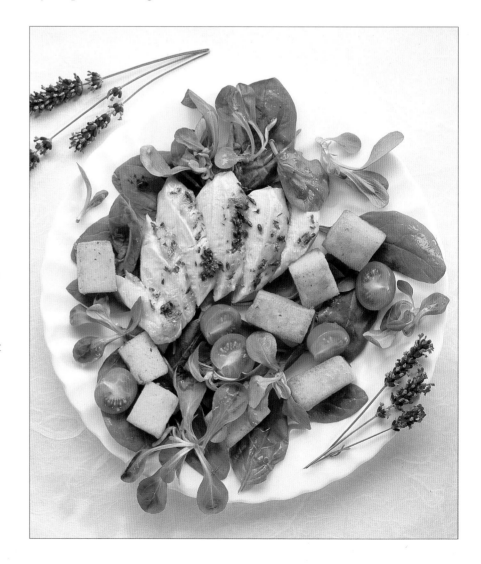

Maryland Salad

Barbecued chicken, corn, bacon, banana and watercress combine here in a sensational main course salad. Serve with baked potatoes and a pat of butter.

INGREDIENTS

Serves 4

4 chicken breasts, boned

8 ounces rindless unsmoked bacon

4 ears corn

3 tablespoons butter, softened

4 ripe bananas, peeled and halved

4 firm tomatoes, halved

1 greenleaf or Boston lettuce

1 bunch watercress

salt and black pepper

For the dressing

5 tablespoons peanut oil

1 tablespoon white wine vinegar

2 teaspoons maple syrup

2 teaspoons mild mustard

1 Season the chicken breasts, brush with oil and barbecue or broil for 15 minutes, turning once. Broil the bacon for 8–10 minutes, or until crisp.

2 Bring a large saucepan of salted water to a boil. Shuck and trim the corn. Boil for 3–5 minutes. For extra flavor, brush with butter and brown over the barbecue or under the broiler. Barbecue or broil the bananas and tomatoes for 6–8 minutes, brushing these with butter too, if you wish.

3 To make the dressing, combine the oil, vinegar, maple syrup and mustard with seasoning and 1 tablespoon water in a screw-top jar and shake well.

4 Wash, spin thoroughly and dress the salad leaves.

5 Distribute the salad leaves among 4 large plates. Slice the chicken and arrange over the leaves with the bacon, banana, corn and tomatoes.

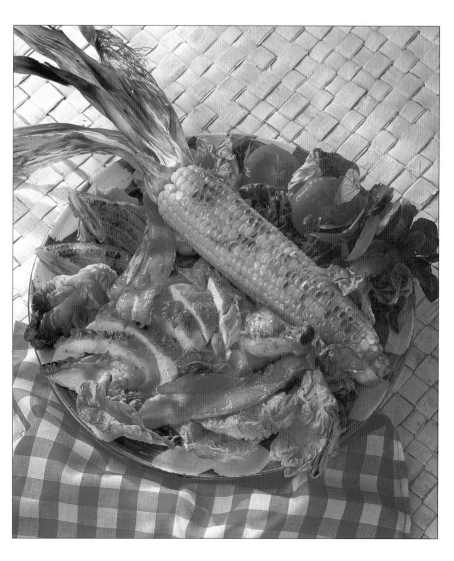

Grilled Chicken with Pica de Gallo Salsa

This dish originated in Mexico. Its hot fruity flavors form the essence of Tex-Mex cooking.

Serves 4

4 chicken breasts

pinch of celery salt and cayenne pepper combined

2 tablespoons vegetable oil

corn chips, to serve

For the salsa

10 ounces watermelon

6 ounces cantaloupe

1 small red onion

1–2 green chilies

2 tablespoons lime juice

4 tablespoons chopped fresh cilantro

pinch of salt

1 Heat the broiler or barbecue to medium. Slash the chicken breasts deeply to speed up the cooking.

2 Season the chicken with the celery salt and cayenne, brush with oil and broil or barbecue for about 15 minutes.

3 To make the salsa, remove the rind and as many seeds as you can from the melons. Finely dice the flesh and put it into a bowl.

4 Finely chop the onion, split the chilies (discarding the seeds, which contain most of the heat) and chop. Take care when handling cut chilies. Mix with the melon.

5 Add the lime juice and cilantro, and season with salt. Put the salsa into a small bowl.

6 Arrange the grilled chicken on a plate and serve with the salsa and a handful of corn chips.

COOK'S TIP

To capture the spirit of Tex-Mex food, cook the chicken over a grill and eat shaded from the hot summer sun.

Coronation Chicken

A summer favorite – serve with a
crisp green salad.

INGREDIENTS

Serves 8

¹/₂ lemon

1 chicken, 5–5¹/₄ pounds

1 onion, quartered

1 carrot, quartered

large bouquet garni

8 black peppercorns, crushed

salt

watercress sprigs, to garnish

For the sauce

1 small onion, chopped

1 tablespoon butter

1 tablespoon curry paste

1 tablespoon tomato paste

¹/₂ cup red wine

1 bay leaf

juice of ¹/₂ lemon, or more to taste

2–3 teaspoons apricot jam

1¹/₄ cups good-quality
    mayonnaise

¹/₂ cup whipping cream, whipped

salt and black pepper

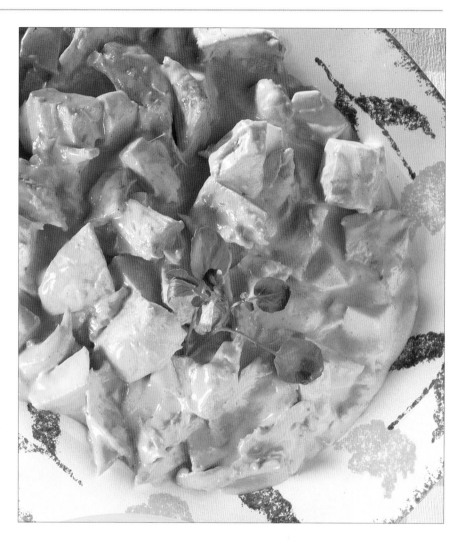

1 Put the lemon half in the chicken cavity, then place the chicken in a saucepan that it just fits. Add the vegetables, bouquet garni, peppercorns and salt.

2 Add enough water to cover two-thirds of the chicken, bring to a boil, then cover and cook gently for 1¹/₂ hours, or until the juices run clear.

3 Transfer to a large bowl, pour the cooking liquid over it and let it cool. Skin and bone the chicken, then chop the flesh.

4 To make the sauce, cook the onion in the butter until soft. Add the curry paste, tomato paste, wine, bay leaf and lemon juice, then cook for 10 minutes. Add the apricot jam; sieve and cool.

5 Beat the sauce into the mayonnaise. Fold in the cream; add seasoning, then stir in the chicken and garnish with watercress.

Peanut Chicken in Pineapple Boats

An impressive-looking dish to serve at a dinner party.

Serves 4

2 small ripe pineapples

1^1/$_2$ cups cooked chicken breast, cut into bite-size pieces

2 stalks celery, diced

3 scallions, white and green parts, chopped

8 ounces seedless green grapes

1^1/$_2$ ounces salted peanuts, coarsely chopped

For the dressing

3 ounces smooth peanut butter

^{1}/$_2$ cup mayonnaise

2 tablespoons cream or milk

1 garlic clove, finely chopped

1 teaspoon mild curry powder

1 tablespoon apricot jam

salt and black pepper

1 Make 4 pineapple boats from the pineapples. Cut the fruit removed from the boats into bite-size pieces.

2 Combine the pineapple flesh, chicken, celery, scallions and grapes in a bowl.

3 Put all the dressing ingredients in another bowl and mix with a wooden spoon or whisk until evenly blended. Season with salt and pepper. (The dressing will be thick, but will be thinned by the juices from the pineapple.)

4 Add the dressing to the pineapple and chicken mixture. Fold together gently but thoroughly.

5 Divide the chicken salad among the pineapple boats. Sprinkle the peanuts over the top before serving.

Warm Chicken and Cilantro Salad

This salad needs to be served warm to make the most of the wonderful sesame and cilantro flavoring. It makes a simple first course or a delicious light lunch dish.

INGREDIENTS

Serves 6

4 medium chicken breasts, boned and skinned

8 ounces snow peas

2 heads decorative lettuce such as red leaf or oakleaf

3 carrots, peeled and cut into small matchsticks

$2^3/_4$ cups button mushrooms, sliced

6 strips bacon, fried, drained on paper towels and crumbled

1 tablespoon chopped fresh cilantro leaves, to garnish

Dressing

$^1/_2$ cup lemon juice

2 tablespoons wholegrain mustard

1 cup olive oil

4 tablespoons sesame oil

1 teaspoon coriander seeds, crushed

1 Mix all the dressing ingredients in a bowl. Place the chicken breasts in a shallow dish and pour on half the dressing. Chill overnight, and store the remaining dressing in the fridge.

2 Cook the snow peas for 2 minutes in boiling water, then cool under cold running water to stop them from cooking any longer. Tear the lettuces into small pieces and mix the other salad ingredients and the bacon together. Arrange all these in individual serving dishes.

3 Broil the chicken breasts until cooked through, then slice them on the diagonal into quite thin pieces. Divide among the bowls of salad, and add some dressing to each dish. Combine quickly and sprinkle some fresh cilantro over each bowl.

Sweet and Sour Kebabs

This marinade contains sugar and will burn very easily, so grill the kebabs slowly, turning often. It is delicious served with Harlequin Rice.

Serves 4

2 chicken breasts, boned and skinned

8 pickling onions or 2 medium onions

4 strips rindless lean bacon

3 firm bananas

1 red bell pepper, seeded and sliced

For the marinade

2 tablespoons light brown sugar

1 tablespoon Worcestershire sauce

2 tablespoons lemon juice

salt and black pepper

For the Harlequin Rice

2 tablespoons olive oil

generous 1 cup cooked rice

1 cup cooked peas

1 small red bell pepper, seeded and diced

1 Mix together the marinade ingredients. Cut each chicken breast into four pieces, add to the marinade, cover and leave for at least 4 hours or preferably overnight in the fridge.

2 Peel the pickling onions, blanch them in boiling water for 5 minutes and drain. If using medium onions, quarter them after blanching.

3 Cut each strip of bacon in half. Peel the bananas and cut each into three pieces. Wrap a strip of bacon around each piece of banana.

4 Thread onto metal skewers with the chicken pieces, onions and pepper slices. Brush with the marinade.

5 Broil or grill over low coals for 15 minutes, turning and basting frequently with the marinade. Keep warm while you prepare the rice.

6 Heat the oil in a frying pan and add the rice, peas and diced pepper. Stir until heated through and serve with the kebabs.

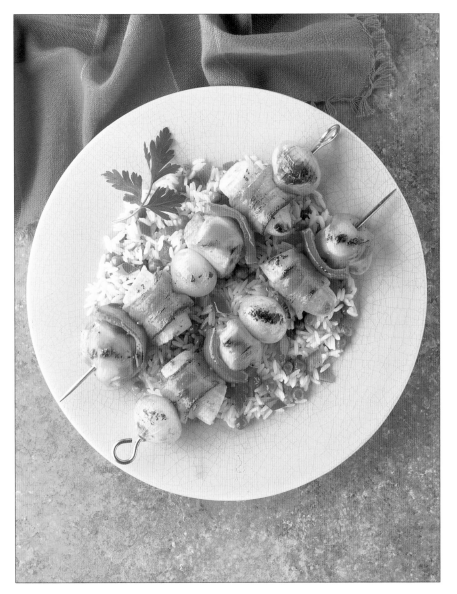

Chicken and Fruit Salad

*The chickens may be cooked a day
before eating, and the salad can be
quickly put together for lunch.*

Serves 8

4 sprigs tarragon or rosemary

2 chickens, 4 pounds each

5 tablespoons softened butter

$^2/_3$ cup homemade or canned
     chicken stock

$^2/_3$ cup white wine

1 cup walnut pieces

1 small cantaloupe

lettuce leaves

1 pound seedless grapes or pitted cherries

salt and black pepper

For the dressing

2 tablespoons tarragon vinegar

$^1/_2$ cup light olive oil

2 tablespoons chopped mixed fresh herbs,
     such as parsley, mint and tarragon

1 Preheat the oven to 400°F. Put
the herb sprigs inside the
chickens and season. Tie the
chickens with string. Spread the
chickens with 4 tablespoons of the
softened butter, place in a roasting
pan and pour in the stock. Cover
loosely with foil and roast for
about 1$^1/_2$ hours, basting twice,
until the skin is browned and the
juices run clear. Remove the
chickens from the roasting pan.

2 Add the wine to the roasting
pan. Bring to a boil and cook
until syrupy. Strain and let cool.
Heat the remaining butter in a
frying pan and gently fry the
walnuts until browned. Drain and
cool. Scoop the melon into balls or
cut into cubes; cut up the chickens.

3 To make the dressing, whisk
the vinegar and oil together
with a little salt and freshly ground
black pepper. Remove all the fat
from the chicken juices and add
these to the dressing with the
herbs. Adjust the seasoning.

4 Arrange the chicken pieces on
a bed of lettuce, sprinkle with
the grapes and melon balls and
spoon on the herb dressing.
Sprinkle with toasted walnuts.

Warm Stir-fried Salad

Warm salads are becoming increasingly popular because they are delicious and nutritious. Arrange the salad leaves on four individual plates, so the hot stir-fry can be served straight from the wok, making sure the lettuce remains crisp and the chicken warm.

INGREDIENTS

Serves 4

2 chicken breasts, about 8 ounces each, boned and skinned

1 tablespoon chopped fresh tarragon

2-inch piece fresh ginger, peeled and finely chopped

3 tablespoons light soy sauce

1 tablespoon sugar

1 tablespoon sunflower oil

1 head Chinese lettuce

$1/2$ frisée lettuce or curly endive, torn into bite-size pieces

1 cup unsalted cashews

2 large carrots, peeled and cut into fine strips

salt and black pepper

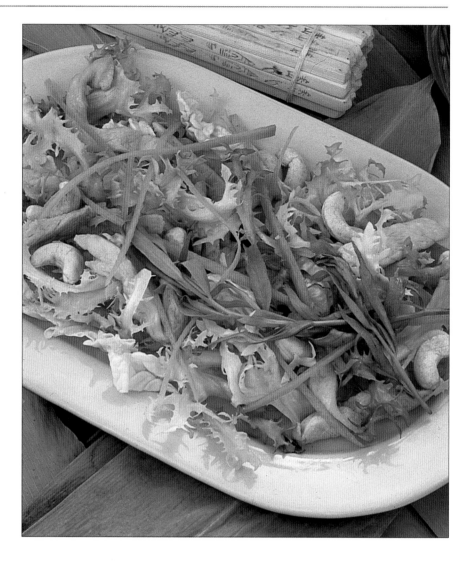

1 Cut the chicken into fine strips and place in a bowl.

2 To make the marinade, mix together in a bowl the tarragon, ginger, soy sauce, sugar and seasoning.

3 Pour the marinade over the chicken strips and marinate for 2–4 hours.

4 Strain the chicken from the marinade, reserving the liquid. Heat a wok or large frying pan, then add the oil. When the oil is hot, stir-fry the chicken for 3 minutes, add the marinade and simmer for 2–3 minutes.

5 Slice the Chinese lettuce and arrange on a plate with the frisée. Toss the cashews and carrots together with the chicken and sauce, pile on top of the bed of lettuce and serve immediately.

Indonesian-style Satay Chicken

Use boneless chicken thighs to give a good flavor to these satays.

INGREDIENTS

Serves 4

$^1/_2$ cup raw peanuts

3 tablespoons vegetable oil

1 small onion, finely chopped

1-inch piece fresh ginger, peeled and finely chopped

1 clove garlic, crushed

$1^1/_2$ pounds chicken thighs, skinned and cut into cubes

$3^1/_2$ ounces creamed coconut, coarsely chopped

1 tablespoon chili sauce

$^1/_4$ cup crunchy peanut butter

1 teaspoon dark brown sugar

$^2/_3$ cup milk

$^1/_4$ teaspoon salt

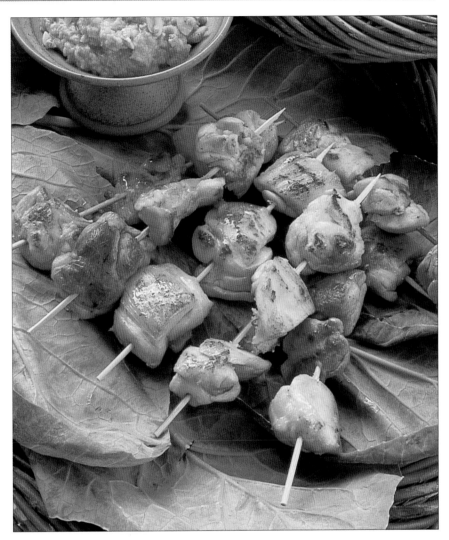

1 Shell and rub the skins from the peanuts, then soak them in a bowl with enough water to cover, for 1 minute. Drain the peanuts and carefully cut them into fine slivers.

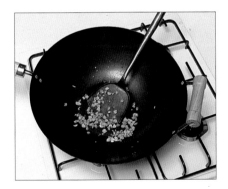

2 Heat a wok or large frying pan and add 1 teaspoon of the oil. When the oil is hot, stir-fry the peanuts for 1 minute, or until crisp and golden. Remove them with a slotted spoon and drain on paper towels.

3 Add the remaining oil to the hot wok. When the oil is hot, add the onion, ginger and garlic and stir-fry for 2–3 minutes, or until softened but not browned. Remove and drain on paper towels.

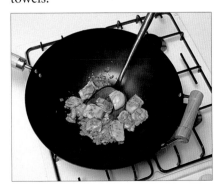

4 Add the chicken and stir-fry for 3–4 minutes, or until crisp on all sides.

5 Thread onto pre-soaked bamboo skewers and keep warm in a low oven.

6 Add the creamed coconut to the hot wok in small pieces and stir-fry until melted. Add the chili sauce, peanut butter and cooked onion, ginger and garlic, and simmer for 2 minutes. Stir in the sugar, milk and salt and simmer for another 3 minutes. Serve the skewered chicken hot, with a dash of the hot dipping sauce sprinkled with the peanuts.

PASTRIES
& PIES

Curried Chicken and Apricot Pie

This sweet and sour pie is unusually enticing. Use boneless turkey instead of chicken, if you wish.

INGREDIENTS

Serves 6

2 tablespoons sunflower oil

1 large onion, chopped

1 pound chicken, boned and roughly chopped

1 tablespoon curry paste or powder

2 tablespoons apricot or peach chutney

$^1/_2$ cup dried apricots, halved

4 ounces cooked carrots, sliced

1 teaspoon mixed dried herbs

4 tablespoons crème fraîche or sour cream

12 ounces ready-made shortcrust pastry

a little egg or milk, to glaze

salt and black pepper

3 Roll out the pastry to 1 inch wider than the pie dish. Cut a strip of pastry from the edge. Damp the rim of the dish, press on the strip, then brush with water and place the sheet of pastry on top, pressing to seal.

4 Preheat the oven to 375°F. Trim any excess pastry and use it to make an attractive pattern on the top, if you wish. Brush all over with beaten egg or milk and bake for 40 minutes, until crisp and golden.

1 Heat the oil in a large pan and fry the onion and chicken until lightly browned. Add the curry paste or powder and fry for another 2 minutes.

2 Add the chutney, apricots, carrots, herbs and crème fraîche to the pan with seasoning. Mix well and then transfer to a deep 5-cup pie dish.

Chicken Pastries with Herb Butter

A herb-coated, buttery chicken fillet wrapped up in crisp pastry.

INGREDIENTS

Serves 4

4 chicken breast fillets, skinned

3/4 cup butter, softened

6 tablespoons chopped mixed fresh herbs, such as thyme, parsley, oregano and rosemary

1 teaspoon lemon juice

5 large sheets filo pastry, defrosted if frozen

1 egg, beaten

2 tablespoons grated Parmesan cheese

salt and black pepper

1 Season the chicken fillets and fry in 2 tablespoons of the butter until lightly browned. Allow to cool.

2 Preheat the oven to 375°F. Put the remaining butter, the herbs, lemon juice and seasoning in a food processor and process until smooth. Melt half the herb butter.

3 Take one sheet of filo pastry and brush with herb butter. Cover the rest of the pastry with a damp dish towel. Fold the pastry sheet in half and brush again with butter. Place a chicken fillet about 1 inch from the top end.

4 Dot the chicken with a quarter of the remaining herb butter. Fold in the sides of the pastry, then roll up to enclose it completely. Place seam-side down on a lightly greased baking sheet. Repeat with the other chicken fillets.

5 Brush the filo pastries with beaten egg. Cut the last sheet of filo into strips, then crumple and arrange on top. Brush them once again with the egg glaze, then sprinkle with Parmesan cheese. Bake for about 35–40 minutes, until golden brown. Serve hot.

Kotopita

This is based on a Greek chicken pie. Serve hot or cold with a typical Greek salad made from tomatoes, cucumber, onions and feta cheese.

INGREDIENTS

Serves 4

10 ounces filo pastry

2 tablespoons olive oil

$1/2$ cup chopped toasted
    almonds

2 tablespoons milk

For the filling

1 tablespoon olive oil

1 medium onion, finely chopped

1 garlic clove, crushed

1 pound cooked chicken, boned

$1/4$ cup crumbled feta cheese

2 eggs, beaten

1 tablespoon chopped fresh
    flat-leaf parsley

1 tablespoon chopped fresh cilantro

1 tablespoon chopped fresh mint

salt and black pepper

1 To make the filling, heat the oil in a large frying pan and cook the chopped onion gently until tender. Add the crushed garlic and cook for another 2 minutes. Transfer to a bowl.

2 Remove the skin from the chicken and grind or chop finely. Add to the onion with the rest of the filling ingredients. Mix thoroughly and season with salt and freshly ground black pepper.

3 Preheat the oven to 375°F. Have a damp dish towel ready to keep the filo pastry covered at all times. You will need to work fast, as the pastry dries out very quickly when exposed to air. Unroll the pastry and cut the whole batch into a 12-inch square.

4 Taking half the sheets (cover the remainder), brush one sheet with a little olive oil, lay it on a well-greased 5-cup oven-proof dish.

5 Sprinkle with a few chopped almonds. Repeat with the other pastry sheets, overlapping them alternately into the dish. Spoon in the filling and cover in the same way with the remaining pastry.

6 Fold in the edges and mark a diamond pattern on the surface with a sharp knife. Brush with milk and sprinkle on the rest of the almonds. Bake for 20–30 minutes, or until golden brown.

Old-fashioned Chicken Pie

The chicken can be roasted and the sauce prepared a day in advance. Allow to cool completely before covering with pastry and baking. Make into four individual pies if you prefer but bake for 10 minutes less.

Serves 4

3–3^1/$_2$ pounds chicken

1 onion, quartered

1 sprig fresh tarragon or rosemary

2 tablespoons butter

1^1/$_2$ cups button mushrooms

2 tablespoons all-purpose flour

1^1/$_4$ cups homemade or canned
   chicken stock

4 ounces cooked ham, diced

2 tablespoons chopped fresh parsley

1 pound frozen puff pastry or pie pastry,
   defrosted

1 egg, beaten

salt and black pepper

1 Preheat the oven to 400°F. Put the chicken into a casserole, along with the quartered onion and the herbs. Add 1^1/$_4$ cups water and season. Cover and roast for about 1^1/$_4$ hours, or until the chicken is tender.

2 Remove the chicken and strain the liquid into a measuring cup. Cool. Remove any fat that settles on the surface. Add enough water to make 1^1/$_4$ cups and reserve for the sauce.

3 Remove the chicken from the bones and cut into large cubes. Melt the butter in a pan, add the mushrooms and cook for 2–3 minutes. Sprinkle in the flour and gradually blend in the stock.

4 Bring to a boil, season to taste and add the ham, chicken and parsley. Turn into a large pie pan and let cool.

5 Roll out the pastry on a lightly floured surface to 2 inches larger than the pie pan. Cut a narrow strip of pastry to place around the edge of the dish. Dampen with a little water and stick to the rim of the dish. Brush the strip with beaten egg.

6 Lay the pastry loosely over the pie, taking care not to stretch it. Press firmly onto the rim. Using a sharp knife, trim away the excess pastry and knock up the sides to encourage the pastry to rise. Crimp the edge neatly and cut a hole in the center of the pie. This allows steam to escape during cooking. Decorate with pastry leaves and chill until ready to bake.

7 Brush the pastry with beaten egg (taking care not to glaze over the sides of the pastry). Bake in the oven for 35–45 minutes, until well risen and nicely browned all over.

Chicken and Mushroom Pie

Use a mixture of dried and fresh mushrooms for this pie.

INGREDIENTS

Serves 6

^{1}/4 cup dried porcini mushrooms

4 tablespoons butter

2 tablespoons all-purpose flour

1 cup chicken stock, warmed

^{1}/4 cup whipping cream or milk

1 onion, coarsely chopped

2 carrots, sliced

2 stalks celery, coarsely chopped

^{3}/4 cup fresh mushrooms, quartered

3 cups cooked chicken meat, cubed

^{1}/2 cup fresh or frozen peas

salt and black pepper

beaten egg, for glazing

For the crust

2 cups all-purpose flour

^{1}/4 teaspoon salt

^{1}/2 cup cold butter, cut into pieces

^{1}/3 cup crisco or vegetable shortening

4–8 tablespoons icewater

1 To make the crust, sift the flour and salt into a bowl. Cut in the butter and shortening until the mixture resembles breadcrumbs. Sprinkle with 6 tablespoons icewater and mix until the dough holds together. Add a little more water, 1 tablespoon at a time if necessary.

2 Gather the dough into a ball and flatten into a disk. Wrap in waxed paper and chill at least 30 minutes.

3 Place the porcini mushrooms in a small bowl. Add hot water to cover and soak until soft, about 30 minutes. Lift out of the water with a slotted spoon, to leave any grit behind, and drain. Discard the soaking water.

4 Preheat the oven to 375°F.

5 Melt 2 tablespoons of the butter in a heavy saucepan. Whisk in the flour and cook until bubbling, whisking constantly. Add the warm stock and cook over medium heat, whisking, until the mixture boils. Cook 2–3 minutes more. Whisk in the cream or milk. Season with salt and pepper. Put to one side.

6 Heat the remaining butter in a large nonstick frying pan until foamy. Add the onion and carrots and cook until softened, about 5 minutes. Add the celery and fresh mushrooms and cook 5 minutes more. Stir in the chicken, peas, and drained porcini mushrooms.

7 Add the chicken mixture to the sauce and stir. Taste for seasoning. Transfer to a rectangular 10-cup baking dish.

8 Roll out the dough to about ^{1}/8 inch thick. Cut out a rectangle about 1 inch larger all around than the dish. Lay the rectangle of dough over the filling. Make a decorative crimped edge by pushing the index finger of one hand between the thumb and index finger of the other.

9 Cut several vents in the top crust to allow steam to escape. Brush with the egg to glaze.

10 Press together the dough trimmings, then roll out again. Cut into strips and lay them over the top crust. Glaze again. If desired, roll small balls of dough and set them in the "windows" in the lattice.

11 Bake until the top crust is browned, about 30 minutes. Serve the pie hot.

Chicken en Croûte

*Chicken breasts, layered with herbs
and orange-flavored stuffing and
wrapped in light puff pastry, make
an impressive dish to serve at a
dinner party.*

INGREDIENTS

Serves 8

1 pound frozen puff pastry, defrosted

4 large chicken breasts, boned and skinned

1 egg, beaten

For the stuffing

1 cup thinly sliced leeks

$^1/_3$ cup chopped lean bacon

2 tablespoons butter

2 cups fresh white breadcrumbs

2 tablespoons chopped fresh herbs, such
    as parsley, thyme, marjoram and chives

grated rind of 1 large orange

1 egg, beaten

salt and black pepper

1 To make the stuffing, cook the
sliced leeks and bacon in the
butter until soft. Put the breadcrumbs into a bowl with the mixed
herbs and plenty of seasoning. Add
the leeks, bacon, butter and the
grated orange rind and bind
together with the beaten egg. If the
mixture is too dry and crumbly,
you can stir in a little orange juice
or chicken stock to bring it to a
moist consistency.

2 Roll out the pastry to a large
rectangle 12 x 16 inches. Trim
the edges and reserve for
decorating the top.

3 Place the chicken breasts
between two pieces of plastic
wrap and flatten to a thickness of
$^1/_4$ inch with a rolling pin. Spread
a third of the leek stuffing over the
center of the pastry. Lay two
chicken breasts side-by-side on top
of the stuffing. Cover the chicken
breasts with another third of the
stuffing, then repeat with the
remaining chicken breasts and the
rest of the stuffing.

4 Make a cut diagonally from
each corner of the pastry to
the chicken. Brush the pastry with
beaten egg.

5 Bring up the sides and overlap
them slightly. Trim away any
excess pastry before folding the
ends over like a package. Turn over
onto a greased baking tray, so that
the seams are underneath. Shape
neatly and trim any excess pastry.

6 With a sharp knife, lightly
criss-cross the pastry into a
diamond pattern. Brush with
beaten egg, and cut leaves from
the trimmings to decorate the top.
Bake at 400°F for 50–60 minutes,
or until well risen and golden
brown on top.

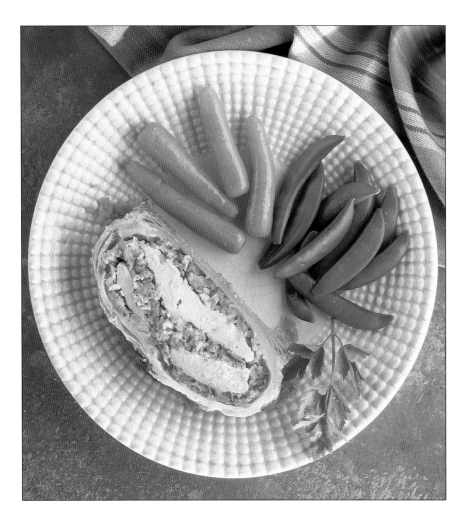

Farmhouse Flan

The lattice pastry topping makes this flan look extra special.

Serves 4

2 cups whole wheat flour

$^1/_4$ cup butter, cubed

$^1/_3$ cup crisco or vegetable shortening

1 teaspoon caraway seeds

1 tablespoon oil

1 onion, chopped

1 garlic clove, crushed

2 cups chopped cooked chicken

$1^1/_2$ cups watercress leaves, chopped

grated rind of $^1/_2$ small lemon

2 eggs, lightly beaten

$^3/_4$ cup heavy or whipping
  cream

3 tablespoons plain yogurt

a good pinch of grated nutmeg

3 tablespoons grated Caerphilly or
  Cheddar cheese

beaten egg, to glaze

salt and black pepper

3 Roll out the pastry and use to line a 7 x 11-inch quiche pan. Reserve the trimmings. Prick the bottom and chill for at least 20 minutes. Place a baking sheet in the oven and preheat it to 400°F.

4 Heat the oil in a frying pan and sauté the onion and garlic for 5–8 minutes, until just softened. Remove from the heat and cool.

5 Line the pastry shell with waxed paper and fill with dried beans. Bake for 10 minutes, then remove the paper and beans and cook for 5 minutes.

6 Mix the onion, garlic, chicken, watercress and lemon rind. Spoon into the pastry shell. Beat the eggs, cream, yogurt, nutmeg, cheese and seasoning and pour. Roll out the pastry trimmings and cut out $^1/_2$-inch strips. Brush with egg, then lay in a lattice pattern over the flan. Press the ends onto the pastry edge. Bake for 35 minutes, or until the top is golden. Serve warm or cold.

1 Place the flour in a bowl with a pinch of salt. Add the butter and shortening and rub into the flour with your fingertips until the mixture resembles breadcrumbs. (Alternatively, you can use a blender or food processor for this.)

2 Stir in the caraway seeds and 3 tablespoons icewater and mix to a firm dough. Knead lightly on a floured surface until smooth.

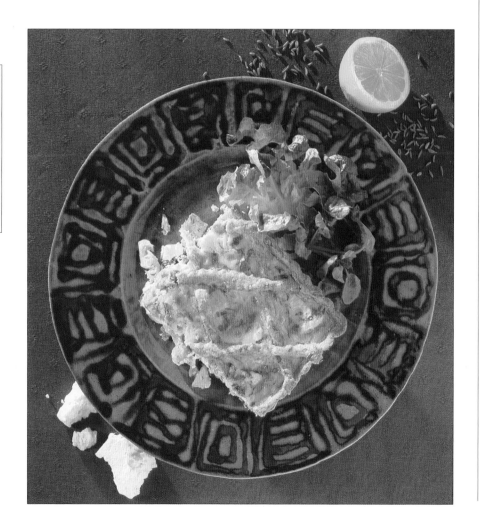

Chicken Charter Pie

Since this dish comes from Cornwall, England, rich heavy cream is used in the filling.

Serves 4

4 tablespoons butter

4 chicken legs

1 onion, finely chopped

$^2/_3$ cup milk

$^2/_3$ cup sour cream

4 scallions, quartered

$^3/_4$ ounce fresh parsley, finely
   chopped

8 ounces frozen puff pastry, defrosted

$^1/_2$ cup heavy cream

2 eggs, beaten, plus extra for glazing

salt and black pepper

1 Melt the butter in a heavy, shallow pan, then brown the chicken legs. Transfer them to a plate.

2 Add the chopped onion to the pan and cook until softened but not browned. Stir the milk, sour cream, scallions, parsley and seasoning into the pan, bring to a boil, then simmer for a couple of minutes.

3 Return the chicken to the pan with any juices, then cover tightly and cook very gently for about 30 minutes. Transfer the chicken and sauce mixture to a deep 5-cup pie pan and allow to cool.

4 Meanwhile, roll out the pastry until about $^3/_4$ inch larger all around than the top of the pie pan. Put the pastry aside while the chicken is cooling.

5 Preheat the oven to 425°F. Cut off a narrow strip around the edge of the pastry, then place the strip on the edge of the pie pan. Moisten the strip, then cover the dish with the pastry. Press the edges together.

6 Make a hole in the center of the pastry and insert a small funnel of foil. Brush the pastry with egg, then bake for 15–20 minutes.

7 Reduce the oven temperature to 350°F. Mix the cream and eggs, then pour into the pie through the funnel. Shake the pie to distribute the cream, then return to the oven for 5–10 minutes. Remove from the oven and let sit in a warm place for 5–10 minutes before serving, or cool completely.

Chicken and Ham Pie

This domed double-crust pie is suitable for a cold buffet, picnics or any packed meals.

INGREDIENTS

Serves 8

14 ounces ready-made shortcrust
    pastry
$1^3/_4$ pounds chicken breasts
12 ounces ham
about $^1/_4$ cup heavy cream
6 scallions, finely chopped
1 tablespoon chopped fresh tarragon
2 teaspoons chopped fresh thyme
grated rind and juice of $^1/_2$ large
    lemon
1 teaspoon freshly ground mace
salt and black pepper
beaten egg or milk, to glaze

1 Preheat the oven to 375°F. Roll out one-third of the pastry and use it to line an 8-inch pie pan. Place on a baking sheet.

2 Grind 4 ounces of the chicken with the ham, then mix with the cream, scallions, herbs, lemon rind, 1 tablespoon of the lemon juice and the seasoning to make a soft mixture; add more cream if necessary.

3 Cut the remaining chicken into $^1/_2$-inch pieces and mix with the remaining lemon juice, the mace and seasoning.

4 Make a layer of one-third of the ham mixture in the pastry shell, cover with half the chopped chicken, then add another layer of one-third of the ham. Add all the remaining chicken followed by the remaining ham mixture.

5 Dampen the edges of the pastry shell. Roll out the remaining two-thirds of the pastry to make a top for the pie.

6 Use the trimmings to make a lattice decoration. Make a small hole in the center of the pie, brush the top with beaten egg or milk, then bake for about 20 minutes. Reduce the oven temperature to 325°F and bake for another 1–$1^1/_4$ hours; cover the top with foil if the pastry becomes too brown. Transfer the pie to a wire rack and let cool.

Chicken, Leek and Parsley Pie

The flavors of chicken and leek complement each other wonderfully.

Serves 4–6
For the pastry
2$^1/_2$ cups all-purpose flour
pinch of salt
scant 1 cup butter, diced
2 egg yolks

For the filling
3 partly boned chicken breasts
flavoring ingredients, such as bouquet
    garni, black peppercorns, onion
    and carrot
4 tablespoons butter
2 leeks, thinly sliced
$^1/_2$ cup grated Cheddar cheese
$^1/_3$ cup finely grated Parmesan cheese
3 tablespoons chopped fresh parsley
2 tablespoons whole-grain mustard
1 teaspoon cornstarch
1$^1/_4$ cups heavy cream
salt and black pepper
beaten egg, to glaze
mixed green salad, to serve

1 To make the pastry, first sift the flour and salt. Blend the butter and egg yolks in a food processor until creamy. Add the flour and process until the mixture is just coming together. Add about 1 tablespoon cold water and process for a few seconds more. Turn out onto a lightly floured surface and knead lightly. Wrap in plastic and chill for about 1 hour.

2 Meanwhile, poach the chicken breasts in water to cover, with the flavoring ingredients added. Cook the chicken until tender. Let cool in the liquid.

3 Preheat the oven to 400°F. Divide the pastry into two pieces, one slightly larger than the other. Roll out the larger piece on a lightly floured surface and use to line a 7 x 11-inch baking dish or pan. Prick the base with a fork and bake for 15 minutes. Set aside to cool.

4 Lift the cooled chicken from the poaching liquid and discard the skins and bones. Cut the chicken into strips. Set aside.

5 Melt the butter in a frying pan and fry the sliced leeks over low heat, stirring occasionally, until soft.

6 Stir in the Cheddar, Parmesan and chopped parsley. Spread half the leek mixture over the cooked pastry shell, leaving a border all the way around.

7 Cover the leek mixture with the chicken strips, then top with the remaining leek mixture. Mix together the whole-grain mustard, cornstarch and cream in a small bowl. Add seasoning to taste. Pour the mixture over the chicken and leek filling.

8 Moisten the edges of the cooked pastry shell. Roll out the remaining pastry into a rectangle and use to cover the pie. Brush the top of the pie with beaten egg and bake in the preheated oven for 30–40 minutes, or until the pie is golden and crisp. Serve hot, cut into generous portions, with a mixed green salad.

Chicken Pastitsio

A traditional Greek pastitsio is a rich, high-fat dish made with ground beef, but this lighter version with chicken is just as tasty.

INGREDIENTS

Serves 4–6

1 pound lean ground chicken

1 large onion, finely chopped

4 tablespoons tomato paste

1 cup red wine or stock

1 teaspoon ground cinnamon

2$^1/_2$ cups macaroni

1$^1/_4$ cups milk

2 tablespoons margarine

4 tablespoons all-purpose flour

1 teaspoon grated nutmeg

2 tomatoes, sliced

4 tablespoons whole-wheat breadcrumbs

salt and black pepper

green salad, to serve

1 Preheat the oven to 425°F. Fry the ground chicken and chopped onion in a nonstick pan without fat, stirring occasionally until lightly browned.

2 Stir in the tomato paste, red wine and cinnamon. Season, then cover and simmer for 5 minutes, stirring occasionally. Remove from the heat.

3 Cook the macaroni in plenty of boiling, salted water until just tender, then drain.

4 Layer the macaroni with the chicken mixture in a wide ovenproof dish.

5 Place the milk, margarine and flour in a saucepan and whisk over medium heat until thickened and smooth. Add the nutmeg and season to taste.

6 Pour the sauce evenly over the pasta and meat layers. Arrange the tomato slices on top and sprinkle whole-wheat breadcrumbs over the surface.

7 Bake for 30–35 minutes, or until golden brown and bubbling. Serve hot with a fresh green salad.

Chicken and Game Pie

A rich filling of chicken and dark meat, spiced with ginger.

INGREDIENTS

Serves 4

1 pound boneless chicken and game meat
   (plus the carcasses and bones)

1 small onion, halved

2 bay leaves

2 carrots, halved

a few black peppercorns

1 tablespoon oil

3 ounces lean bacon, rinded and
   chopped

1 tablespoon all-purpose flour

3 tablespoons sweet sherry or Madeira

2 teaspoons ground ginger

grated rind and juice of $1/2$ orange

12 ounces frozen puff pastry, defrosted

beaten egg or milk, to glaze

salt and black pepper

1 Place the carcasses and bones in a pan, with any giblets and half the onion, the bay leaves, carrots and black peppercorns. Cover with water and bring to a boil. Simmer until reduced to about $1^1/4$ cups, then strain the stock.

2 Cut the chicken and game meat into even-size pieces. Chop the remaining onion, then fry in the oil until softened. Then add the bacon and meat and fry for a few minutes. Sprinkle on the flour and stir until beginning to brown. Gradually add the stock, stirring as it thickens, then add the sherry or Madeira, ginger, orange rind and juice, and seasoning. Simmer for 20 minutes.

3 Transfer to a 4-cup pie pan and allow to cool slightly. Use a pie funnel to help hold up the pastry.

4 Preheat the oven to 425°F. Roll out the pastry to 1 inch larger than the dish. Cut off a $1/2$-inch strip all around. Dampen the rim of the pan and press on the strip of pastry. Dampen again and then lift the pastry carefully over the pie, sealing the edges well at the rim. Trim off the excess pastry, use to decorate the top, then brush the pie with egg or milk.

5 Bake the pie for 15 minutes, then reduce the oven temperature to 375°F and bake for another 25–30 minutes.

Chicken and Stilton Pies

These individual pies are wrapped in crisp pie crust and shaped into pastries. They are great for lunch, served hot or cold.

INGREDIENTS

Makes 4

3 cups self-rising flour

$^1/_2$ teaspoon salt

6 tablespoons crisco or vegetable
   shortening

6 tablespoons butter

4–5 tablespoons cold water

beaten egg, to glaze

For the filling

1 pound chicken thighs, boned and
   skinned

$^1/_4$ cup chopped walnuts

1 ounce scallions, sliced

$^1/_2$ cup Stilton, crumbled

1 ounce celery, finely chopped

$^1/_2$ teaspoon dried thyme

salt and black pepper

3 Remove any fat from the chicken thighs and cut into small cubes. Mix with the chopped walnuts, scallions, Stilton, celery, thyme and seasoning and divide the filling equally among the four pastry circles.

4 Brush the edge of the pastry with beaten egg and fold over, pinching and crimping the edges together well. Place on a greased baking sheet and bake in the oven for about 45 minutes, or until golden brown.

1 Preheat the oven to 400°F. Mix the flour and salt in a bowl. Rub in the shortening and butter with your fingers until the mixture resembles fine breadcrumbs. Using a knife to cut and stir, mix in the cold water to form a stiff, pliable dough.

2 Turn out onto a work surface and knead lightly until smooth. Divide into four portions and roll out each piece to a thickness of $^1/_4$ inch. Cut into an 8-inch circle.

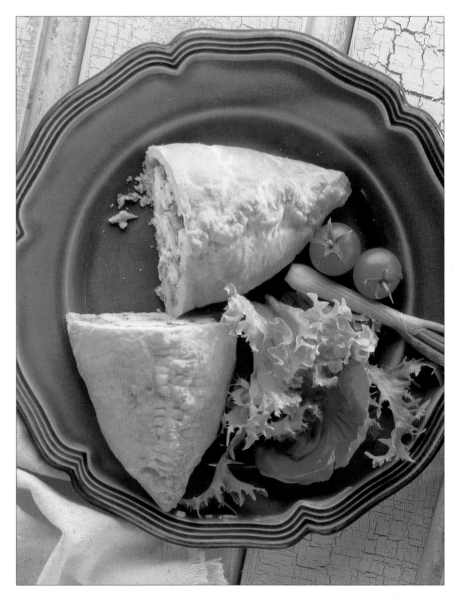

Chicken Bouche

A spectacular centerpiece, this light pastry shell contains a delicious chicken and mushroom filling with a hint of fruit. Ideal served with freshly cooked vegetables.

INGREDIENTS

Serves 4

1 pound frozen puff pastry, defrosted

beaten egg, to glaze

For the filling

1 tablespoon oil

3 cups ground chicken

4 tablespoons all-purpose flour

$^2/_3$ cup milk

$^2/_3$ cup homemade or canned
   chicken stock

4 scallions, chopped

$^1/_4$ cup redcurrants or raspberries

1 cup button mushrooms, sliced

1 tablespoon chopped fresh tarragon

salt and black pepper

1 Preheat the oven to 400°F. Roll half the pastry out on a lightly floured work surface to a 10-inch oval. Roll out the remainder to an oval of the same size and draw a smaller 8-inch oval in the center.

2 Brush the edge of the first pastry shape with the beaten egg and place the smaller oval on top. Place on a dampened baking sheet and bake for 30 minutes.

3 For the filling, heat the oil in a large pan. Fry the ground chicken for 5 minutes. Add the flour and cook for another minute. Stir in the milk and stock and bring to a boil.

4 Add the scallions, redcurrants and mushrooms. Cook for 20 minutes.

5 Stir in the fresh tarragon and season to taste.

6 Place the pastry bouche on a serving plate, remove the oval center and spoon in the filling. Place the oval lid on top. Serve with freshly cooked vegetables.

VARIATION

You can also use regular pie pastry for this dish and cook as a traditional chicken pie.

HOT & SPICY

Simple Curried Chicken

A tasty curry that needs very little preparation.

INGREDIENTS

Serves 4

2 tablespoons vegetable oil

1 onion, chopped

1 green or red bell pepper, seeded
   and diced

1 garlic clove, finely chopped

1^1/$_2$ tablespoons curry powder

^{1}/$_2$ teaspoon dried thyme

1 pound tomatoes, skinned, seeded and
   chopped, or canned chopped tomatoes

2 tablespoons lemon juice

^{1}/$_2$ cup water

2 ounces currants or raisins

salt and black pepper

1 chicken, 3–3^1/$_2$ pounds, skinned and
   cut into 8 pieces

cooked rice, to serve

1 Preheat the oven to 350°F. Heat the vegetable oil in a wide, deep frying pan that has a lid and an ovenproof handle or in a flame-proof casserole. Add the chopped onion, diced bell pepper and garlic. Cook, stirring occasionally, until the vegetables are soft.

2 Stir in the curry powder and thyme, then add the tomatoes, lemon juice and water. Bring the sauce to a boil, stirring frequently. Stir in the currants or raisins. Season to taste.

3 Put the chicken pieces in the frying pan or casserole, arranging them in one layer. Turn them, so that they are thoroughly coated with the sauce. Cover the pan and transfer to the oven. Cook for about 40 minutes, or until the chicken is tender. Turn the pieces halfway through cooking to keep coated in sauce.

4 Transfer the chicken and sauce to a warmed serving platter. Serve with freshly boiled rice.

VARIATION

For Curried Chicken Casserole, a slightly hotter dish, omit the diced bell pepper and cook 1^1/$_2$ tablespoons finely chopped fresh ginger and 1 green chili, seeded and finely chopped, with the onion and garlic in a flameproof casserole. In step 2, stir in the curry powder with 1^3/$_4$ cups plain yogurt; omit the tomatoes, lemon juice and water. Add the chicken pieces, cover and bake at 325°F for 1–1^1/$_4$ hours, or until the chicken is very tender.

Tangy Chicken

*There are few cooking concepts that
are better suited to today's busy
lifestyle than the all-in-one stir-fry.
This delicious example has a
Southeast Asian influence.*

INGREDIENTS

Serves 4

10 ounces Chinese egg noodles

2 tablespoons vegetable oil

3 scallions, chopped

1 garlic clove, crushed

1-inch piece fresh ginger, peeled
    and grated

1 teaspoon hot paprika

1 teaspoon ground coriander

3 chicken breasts, boned and
    sliced

1 cup sugar-snap peas, trimmed

4 ounces baby corn, halved

8 ounces fresh beansprouts

1 tablespoon cornstarch

3 tablespoons soy sauce

3 tablespoons lemon juice

1 tablespoon sugar

3 tablespoons chopped fresh cilantro
    or scallion tops, to garnish

1 Bring a large saucepan of salted
water to a boil. Add the egg
noodles and cook according to the
instructions on the package. Drain,
cover and keep warm.

2 Heat the oil in a wok or large
frying pan. Add the scallions
and cook over low heat. Mix in the
next five ingredients, then stir-fry
for 3–4 minutes. Add the next
three ingredients and steam briefly.
Add the noodles.

3 Combine the cornstarch, soy
sauce, lemon juice and sugar in
a small bowl. Add to the wok or
pan and simmer briefly to thicken.
Serve garnished with chopped
cilantro or scallion tops.

Chicken with Pineapple

This chicken has a delicate tang and is very tender. The pineapple not only tenderizes the chicken but also gives it a slight sweetness.

INGREDIENTS

Serves 6

8-ounce can pineapple chunks

1 teaspoon ground cumin

1 teaspoon ground coriander

$^1/_2$ teaspoon crushed garlic

1 teaspoon ground chilies

1 teaspoon salt

2 tablespoons plain yogurt

1 tablespoon chopped fresh cilantro

orange food coloring (optional)

10 ounces chicken, skinned and boned

$^1/_2$ red bell pepper

$^1/_2$ yellow or green bell pepper

1 large onion

6 cherry tomatoes

1 tablespoon vegetable oil

1 Drain the pineapple juice into a bowl. Reserve 8 large chunks of pineapple, squeeze the juice from the remaining chunks into the bowl and set aside. You should have about $^1/_2$ cup pineapple juice.

2 In a large mixing bowl, blend the cumin, ground coriander, garlic, ground chili, salt, yogurt, fresh cilantro and a few drops of food coloring, if using. Pour the reserved pineapple juice into the mixture and stir.

3 Cut the chicken into bite-size cubes, add to the mixing bowl with the yogurt and spice mixture and allow to marinate for about 1–1$^1/_2$ hours.

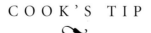

4 Cut the peppers and onion into bite-size chunks.

> ### COOK'S TIP
> ❧
>
> If possible, use a mixture of chicken breast and thigh meat for this recipe.

5 Preheat the broiler to medium. Arrange the chicken pieces, peppers, onion, tomatoes and reserved pineapple chunks alternately on 6 wooden or metal skewers.

6 Baste the kebabs with the oil, then place the skewers on a flameproof dish or broiler pan. Broil, turning and basting the chicken pieces with the marinade regularly, for about 15 minutes.

7 Once the chicken pieces are cooked, remove them from the broiler and serve either with salad or plain boiled rice.

Chicken with Spiced Rice

This is a good dish for entertaining. It can be prepared in advance and reheated in the oven. Serve with traditional curry accompaniments.

Serves 8

2 pounds boneless chicken thighs

4 tablespoons olive oil

2 large onions, thinly sliced

1–2 green chilies, seeded and finely chopped

1 teaspoon grated fresh ginger

1 garlic clove, crushed

1 tablespoon hot curry powder

$^2/_3$ cup homemade or canned chicken stock

$^2/_3$ cup plain yogurt

2 tablespoons chopped fresh cilantro, to garnish

salt and black pepper

For the spiced rice

generous $2^1/_4$ cups white basmati rice

$^1/_2$ teaspoon garam masala

$3^3/_4$ cups chicken stock or water

scant $^1/_2$ cup dark or golden raisins

$^1/_2$ cup chopped toasted almonds

1 Put the basmati rice into a sieve and wash under cold running water to remove any starchy powder coating the grains. Then put into a bowl, cover with cold water and let soak for 30 minutes. The grains will absorb some water so that they will not stick together in a solid mass while cooking.

2 Preheat the oven to 325°F. Cut the chicken into bite-size cubes. Heat 2 tablespoons of the oil in a large flameproof casserole, add one onion and cook until softened. Add the finely chopped chilies, grated ginger, crushed garlic and curry powder to the casserole and continue cooking for another 2 minutes, stirring occasionally.

3 Add the stock and seasoning, and bring slowly to a boil. Add the chicken. Cover and bake for 20 minutes, or until tender.

4 Remove from the oven and stir in the yogurt.

5 Meanwhile, heat the remaining oil in a flameproof casserole and cook the remaining onion gently until tender and lightly browned. Add the drained rice, garam masala and stock or water. Bring to a boil, cover and cook in the oven with the chicken for 20–35 minutes, or until the rice is tender and all the stock has been absorbed.

6 To serve, stir the raisins and toasted almonds into the rice. Spoon half the rice into a large deep serving dish, cover with the chicken and then the remaining rice. Sprinkle with chopped cilantro to garnish.

Hot Chicken Curry

This curry has a delicious thick sauce with extra color provided by chunks of red and green pepper.

INGREDIENTS

Serves 4

2 tablespoons corn oil

$^{1}/_{4}$ teaspoon fenugreek seeds

$^{1}/_{4}$ teaspoon onion seeds

2 onions, chopped

$^{1}/_{2}$ teaspoon chopped garlic

$^{1}/_{2}$ teaspoon chopped fresh ginger

1 teaspoon ground coriander

1 teaspoon ground chilies

1 teaspoon salt

14-ounce can tomatoes

2 tablespoons lemon juice

$2^{1}/_{2}$ cups cubed chicken

2 tablespoons chopped fresh cilantro

3 green chilies, chopped

$^{1}/_{2}$ red bell pepper, cut into chunks

$^{1}/_{2}$ green bell pepper, cut into chunks

fresh cilantro sprigs, to garnish

1 In a medium saucepan, heat the oil and fry the fenugreek and onion seeds until they turn a shade darker. Add the chopped onions, garlic and ginger and fry for about 5 minutes, until the onions turn golden brown. Reduce the heat to very low.

COOK'S TIP

∼

For a milder version of this delicious curry, simply omit some or all of the green chilies.

2 Meanwhile, in a separate bowl, combine the ground coriander, ground chilies, salt, tomatoes and lemon juice.

3 Pour this mixture into the saucepan with the onions and increase the heat to medium. Stir-fry for about 3 minutes.

4 Add the chicken pieces and stir-fry for 5–7 minutes.

5 Add the cilantro, chilies and peppers. Lower the heat, cover and simmer for 10 minutes, until the chicken is cooked.

6 Serve hot, garnished with fresh cilantro sprigs.

San Francisco Chicken Wings

Make these as spicy as you like – just add more chili sauce.

INGREDIENTS

Serves 4

3/4 cup soy sauce

1 tablespoon light brown sugar

1 tablespoon rice vinegar

2 tablespoons dry sherry

juice of 1 orange

2-inch strip orange rind

1 star anise

1 teaspoon cornstarch

1/4 cup water

1 tablespoon minced fresh ginger

1/4–1 teaspoon Asian chili-garlic
   sauce, to taste

3–3 1/2 pounds chicken wings, about
   22–24, tips removed

1 Preheat the oven to 400°F. In a saucepan, combine the soy sauce, light brown sugar, rice vinegar, dry sherry, orange juice and rind and star anise. Bring to a boil over a medium heat.

2 Combine the cornstarch and water in a small bowl and stir until blended. Add to the boiling soy sauce mixture, stirring well. Boil for another 1 minute, stirring constantly.

3 Remove the soy sauce mixture from the heat and stir in the minced ginger and chili-garlic sauce to taste.

4 Arrange the chicken wings in one layer in a large baking dish. Pour the soy sauce mixture over them and stir to coat the wings.

5 Bake until tender and browned, 30–40 minutes, basting occasionally. Serve the wings hot or warm.

Fragrant Chicken Curry

In this dish, the mildly spiced sauce is thickened using lentils rather than the traditional onions fried in ghee.

INGREDIENTS

Serves 4

scant $^1/_2$ cup red lentils

2 tablespoons mild curry powder

2 teaspoons ground coriander

1 teaspoon cumin seeds

2 cups vegetable stock

8 chicken thighs, skinned

8 ounces shredded fresh or thawed frozen
    spinach, well drained

1 tablespoon chopped fresh cilantro

salt and black pepper

fresh cilantro sprigs, to garnish

white or brown basmati rice and
    poppadums, to serve

1 Rinse the lentils under cold running water. Put into a large, heavy saucepan with the curry powder, ground coriander, cumin seeds and stock.

2 Bring to a boil, then lower the heat. Cover and simmer gently for 10 minutes.

3 Add the chicken and spinach. Cover and simmer gently for another 40 minutes, or until the chicken is cooked.

4 Stir in the chopped cilantro and season to taste. Serve garnished with cilantro sprigs and accompanied by the rice and poppadums.

Spicy Masala Chicken

These chicken pieces are broiled and have a sweet-and-sour taste. They can be served cold with a salad and rice or hot with mashed potatoes.

INGREDIENTS

Serves 6

12 chicken thighs

6 tablespoons lemon juice

1 teaspoon chopped fresh ginger

1 teaspoon chopped garlic

1 teaspoon crushed dried red chilies

1 teaspoon salt

1 teaspoon light brown sugar

2 tablespoons honey

2 tablespoons chopped fresh cilantro

1 green chili, finely chopped

2 tablespoons vegetable oil

fresh cilantro sprigs, to garnish

1 Prick the chicken thighs with a fork, rinse, pat dry and set aside in a bowl.

2 In a large mixing bowl, make the marinade by combining the lemon juice, ginger, garlic, crushed dried red chilies, salt, sugar and honey.

3 Transfer the chicken thighs to the spice mixture and coat well. Set aside for about 45 minutes.

4 Preheat the broiler to medium. Add the cilantro and chopped green chili to the chicken thighs and place them in a flameproof baking dish.

5 Pour any remaining marinade over the chicken and baste with the oil.

6 Broil the chicken thighs under the preheated broiler for 15–20 minutes, turning and basting occasionally, until they are cooked through and browned.

7 Transfer the chicken to a serving dish and garnish with a few sprigs of cilantro.

Tandoori Chicken

A famous Indian/Pakistani chicken dish which is cooked in, and takes its name from, a clay oven called a tandoor, this is extremely popular in the West and appears on the majority of Indian restaurant menus. Though the authentic tandoori flavor is difficult to achieve in conventional ovens, this version still makes a very tasty dish.

INGREDIENTS

Serves 4

4 chicken quarters

3/4 cup plain low-fat yogurt

1 teaspoon garam masala

1 teaspoon chopped fresh ginger

1 teaspoon chopped garlic

1 1/2 teaspoons ground chilies

1/4 teaspoon ground turmeric

1 teaspoon ground coriander

1 tablespoon lemon juice

1 teaspoon salt

a few drops red food coloring

2 tablespoons corn oil

To garnish

mixed lettuce leaves

lime wedges

1 tomato, quartered

1 Skin, rinse and pat dry the chicken quarters. Make 2 slits in the flesh of each piece, place in a dish and set aside.

2 Stir together the yogurt, garam masala, ginger, garlic, ground chilies, turmeric, ground coriander, lemon juice, salt, red food coloring and oil, and beat until well mixed.

3 Cover the chicken quarters with the yogurt and spice mixture and marinate for about 3 hours.

4 Preheat the oven to 475°F. Transfer the chicken pieces to an ovenproof dish.

5 Bake in the oven for 20–25 minutes, or until the chicken is cooked through and browned on top.

6 Remove from the oven, transfer to a serving dish and garnish with the lettuce leaves, lime and tomato.

Chicken Naan Pockets

This quick and easy dish is ideal for a speedy snack, lunch or supper. To save time, use the ready-to-bake naans available in some supermarkets and Asian stores, or try warmed pita bread instead.

INGREDIENTS

Serves 4

4 ready-prepared naans

3 tablespoons plain low-fat yogurt

$1^1/2$ teaspoons garam masala

1 teaspoon ground chilies

1 teaspoon salt

3 tablespoons lemon juice

1 tablespoon chopped fresh cilantro

1 green chili, chopped

$3^1/4$ cups cubed chicken

1 tablespoon vegetable oil (optional)

8 onion rings

2 tomatoes, quartered

$^1/2$ white cabbage, shredded

To garnish

lemon wedges

2 small tomatoes, halved

mixed lettuce leaves

fresh cilantro

1 Cut into the middle of each naan to make a pocket, then set aside.

2 Stir together the yogurt, garam masala, ground chilies, salt, lemon juice, fresh cilantro and chopped green chili. Pour the marinade over the chicken pieces and allow to marinate for about 1 hour.

3 Preheat the broiler to very hot, then lower the heat to medium. Place the chicken in a flameproof dish and broil for 15–20 minutes, until cooked, turning the chicken pieces at least twice.

4 Remove from the heat and fill each naan with the chicken, onion rings, tomatoes and cabbage. Serve with the garnish ingredients.

Chicken Tikka

This chicken dish is an extremely popular Indian appetizer and is quick and easy to cook. Chicken Tikka can also be served as a main course for four.

INGREDIENTS

Serves 6

$3^1/4$ cups cubed chicken

1 teaspoon chopped fresh ginger

1 teaspoon chopped garlic

1 teaspoon ground chilies

$^1/4$ teaspoon ground turmeric

1 teaspoon salt

$^2/3$ cup plain low-fat yogurt

4 tablespoons lemon juice

1 tablespoon chopped fresh cilantro

1 tablespoon vegetable oil

To garnish

1 small onion, cut into rings

lime wedges

mixed salad

fresh cilantro

1 In a medium bowl, combine the chicken pieces, ginger, garlic, ground chilies, turmeric, salt, yogurt, lemon juice and fresh cilantro and marinate for at least 2 hours.

2 Place on a broiler pan or in a flameproof dish lined with foil and baste with the oil.

3 Preheat the broiler to medium. Broil the chicken for 15–20 minutes, until cooked, turning and basting two or three times. Serve with the garnish ingredients.

Chicken in Cashew Sauce

This chicken dish has a deliciously thick and nutty sauce, and it is best served with plain boiled rice.

INGREDIENTS

Serves 4

2 onions

2 tablespoons tomato paste

^{1}/$_3$ cup cashews

1^1/$_2$ teaspoons garam masala

1 teaspoon crushed garlic

1 teaspoon ground chilies

1 tablespoon lemon juice

^{1}/$_4$ teaspoon ground turmeric

1 teaspoon salt

1 tablespoon plain low-fat yogurt

2 tablespoons corn oil

1 tablespoon chopped fresh cilantro

1 tablespoon golden raisins

3^1/$_4$ cups cubed chicken

2^1/$_4$ cups button mushrooms

1^1/$_4$ cups water

chopped fresh cilantro, to garnish

1 Cut the onions into quarters, then place them in a food processor or blender and process for about 1 minute.

2 Add the tomato paste, cashews, garam masala, garlic, ground chilies, lemon juice, turmeric, salt and yogurt. Process for another 1–1^1/$_2$ minutes.

3 In a saucepan, heat the oil, lower the heat to medium and pour in the spice mixture from the food processor. Fry for about 2 minutes, turning down the heat if necessary.

4 Add the fresh cilantro, golden raisins and cubed chicken and continue to stir-fry for 1 minute.

5 Add the mushrooms, pour in the water and bring to a simmer. Cover and cook over low heat for about 10 minutes, or until the chicken is cooked through and the sauce is thick. Cook for a little longer if necessary.

6 Serve garnished with chopped fresh cilantro.

Chicken with Green Mango

Green, unripe mango is used for cooking various dishes on the Indian sub-continent, including pickles, chutneys and some meat, chicken and vegetable dishes. This is a fairly simple chicken dish to prepare and is served with rice and dal.

INGREDIENTS

Serves 4

1 green mango

3¹/₄ cups cubed chicken

¹/₄ teaspoon black onion seeds

1 teaspoon grated fresh ginger

¹/₂ teaspoon crushed garlic

1 teaspoon ground chilies

¹/₄ teaspoon ground turmeric

1 teaspoon salt

1 teaspoon ground coriander

2 tablespoons corn oil

2 onions, sliced

4 curry leaves

1¹/₄ cups water

2 tomatoes, quartered

2 green chilies, chopped

2 tablespoons chopped fresh cilantro

1 To prepare the mango, peel, pit and slice the flesh thickly. Place the mango slices in a small bowl, cover and set aside.

2 Place the chicken cubes in a bowl and add the onion seeds, ginger, garlic, ground chilies, turmeric, salt and ground coriander. Mix the spices into the chicken and then add half the mango slices.

3 In a medium saucepan, heat the oil and fry the sliced onions until they turn golden brown. Add the curry leaves.

4 Gradually add the spiced chicken pieces and mango slices, stirring constantly.

5 Pour in the water, lower the heat and cook for about 12–15 minutes, stirring occasionally, until the chicken is cooked through and the water has been absorbed.

6 Add the remaining mango slices, the tomatoes, green chilies and cilantro and serve hot.

Karahi Chicken with Mint

For this tasty dish, the chicken is first boiled before being quickly stir-fried in a little oil.

INGREDIENTS

INGREDIENTS

Serves 4

10 ounces chicken breast fillet, skinned
   and cut into strips

1¼ cups water

2 tablespoons soy oil

2 bunches scallions, coarsely chopped

1 teaspoon grated fresh ginger

1 teaspoon crushed dried red chili

2 tablespoons lemon juice

1 tablespoon chopped fresh cilantro

1 tablespoon chopped fresh mint

3 tomatoes, seeded and
   roughly chopped

1 teaspoon salt

mint and cilantro sprigs, to garnish

1 Put the chicken and water into a saucepan, bring to a boil and lower the heat to medium. Cook for about 10 minutes, or until the water has evaporated and the chicken is cooked. Remove from the heat and set aside.

2 Heat the oil in a frying pan or saucepan and stir-fry the scallions for about 2 minutes until soft.

3 Add the boiled chicken strips to the frying pan or saucepan and stir-fry them for about 3 minutes over medium heat.

4 Gradually add the ginger, dried chili, lemon juice, fresh cilantro, fresh mint, tomatoes and salt and gently stir to blend all the flavors together well.

5 Transfer to a serving dish and garnish with the fresh mint and cilantro sprigs.

Karahi Chicken with Fresh Fenugreek

Fresh fenugreek is a flavor that is not widely known. This recipe is a good introduction to this delicious herb.

INGREDIENTS

Serves 4

4 ounces chicken thigh meat, skinned and cut into strips

4 ounces chicken breast fillet, cut into strips

$^1/_2$ teaspoon chopped garlic

1 teaspoon ground chilies

$^1/_2$ teaspoon salt

2 teaspoons tomato paste

2 tablespoons soy oil

1 bunch fenugreek leaves

1 tablespoon chopped fresh cilantro

$1^1/_4$ cups water

rice or chapatis, to serve

1 Bring a saucepan of water to a boil, add the chicken and cook for 5–7 minutes. Drain.

2 In a mixing bowl, combine the garlic, ground chilies and salt with the tomato paste.

3 Heat the oil in a large saucepan. Lower the heat and add the tomato paste and spice mixture.

4 Add the chicken pieces and stir-fry for 5–7 minutes. Lower the heat again.

5 Add the fenugreek leaves and fresh cilantro. Continue to stir-fry for 5–7 minutes.

6 Pour in the water, cover and cook for about 5 minutes, and serve hot with rice or chapatis.

COOK'S TIP

When preparing fresh fenugreek, use only the leaves and discard the stems, which are very bitter.

Moroccan Chicken Couscous

A subtly spiced and fragrant dish with a fruity sauce.

INGREDIENTS

Serves 4

1 tablespoon butter

1 tablespoon sunflower oil

4 chicken portions, about 6 ounces each

2 onions, finely chopped

2 garlic cloves, crushed

$1/2$ teaspoon ground cinnamon

$1/4$ teaspoon ground ginger

$1/4$ teaspoon ground turmeric

2 tablespoons orange juice

2 teaspoons honey

salt

fresh mint sprigs, to garnish

For the couscous

2 cups couscous

1 teaspoon salt

2 teaspoons sugar

2 tablespoons sunflower oil

$1/2$ teaspoon ground cinnamon

pinch of grated nutmeg

1 tablespoon orange flower water

2 tablespoons golden raisins

$1/2$ cup chopped blanched almonds

3 tablespoons chopped pistachios

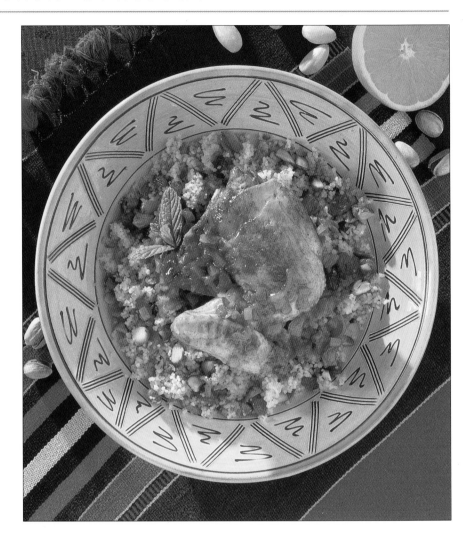

1 Heat the butter and oil in a large pan and add the chicken portions, skin-side down. Fry for 3–4 minutes, until the skin is golden, then turn over.

2 Add the onions, garlic, spices and a pinch of salt and pour on the orange juice and $1^{1}/4$ cups water. Cover and bring to a boil, then reduce the heat and simmer for about 30 minutes.

3 Meanwhile, place the couscous and salt in a bowl and cover with $1^{1}/2$ cups water. Stir once and let stand for 5 minutes. Add the sugar, 1 tablespoon of the oil, the cinnamon, nutmeg, orange flower water and golden raisins and mix.

4 Heat the remaining 1 tablespoon oil in a pan and lightly fry the almonds until golden. Stir into the couscous with the pistachios.

5 Line a steamer with waxed paper and spoon in the couscous. Sit the steamer over the chicken (or over a pan of boiling water) and steam for 10 minutes.

6 Remove the steamer and keep covered. Stir the honey into the chicken liquid and boil rapidly for 3–4 minutes. Spoon the couscous onto a warmed serving platter. Top with the chicken, and some of the sauce. Garnish with the fresh mint and serve with the remaining sauce.

Chicken and Chorizo Tacos

Use ready-made taco shells and fill with tasty ground chicken.

INGREDIENTS

Serves 4

1 tablespoon vegetable oil

1 pound ground chicken

1 teaspoon salt

1 teaspoon ground cumin

12 taco shells

3 ounces chorizo sausage, chopped

3 scallions, chopped

2 tomatoes, chopped

$^1/_2$ head of lettuce, shredded

2 cups grated Cheddar cheese

tomato salsa, to serve

1 Preheat the oven to 350°F.

2 Heat the oil in a nonstick frying pan. Add the chicken, salt and cumin and fry over medium heat until the chicken is cooked through, 5–8 minutes. Stir frequently to prevent large lumps from forming.

3 Meanwhile, arrange the taco shells in one layer on a large baking sheet and heat in the oven for about 10 minutes, or according to the directions on the package.

4 Add the chorizo and scallions to the chicken and stir to combine. Cook until just warmed through, stirring occasionally.

5 To assemble each taco, place 1–2 spoonfuls of the chicken mixture in the bottom of a warmed taco shell. Top with a generous sprinkling of chopped tomato, shredded lettuce, and grated cheese.

6 Serve immediately, with tomato salsa to accompany.

Chicken Pilaf

This dish is a complete meal in itself, but also makes a good accompaniment to curries.

INGREDIENTS

INGREDIENTS

Serves 4

2 cups basmati rice

6 tablespoons low-fat margarine

1 onion, sliced

$1/4$ teaspoon mixed black onion and mustard seeds

3 curry leaves

1 teaspoon grated fresh ginger

1 teaspoon crushed garlic

1 teaspoon ground coriander

1 teaspoon ground chilies

$1^{1}/2$ teaspoons salt

2 tomatoes, sliced

1 potato, cubed

$1/2$ cup frozen peas

$1^{1}/4$ cups cubed chicken

4 tablespoons chopped fresh cilantro

2 green chilies, chopped

3 cups water

1 Wash and soak the rice in cold water for 30 minutes, then set aside in a sieve.

2 In a medium saucepan, melt the low-fat margarine and fry the sliced onion until golden.

3 Add the onion and mustard seeds, the curry leaves, grated ginger, crushed garlic, ground coriander, ground chilies and salt to the saucepan. Stir-fry for about 2 minutes to cook the spices.

4 Add the sliced tomatoes, cubed potato, peas and chicken and mix well.

5 Add the drained rice and stir gently to combine with the other ingredients.

6 Finally, add the fresh cilantro and chopped green chilies. Mix and stir-fry for another minute. Pour in the water.

7 Bring to a boil and lower the heat. Cover and cook for about 20 minutes.

Cajun Chicken

Use ham and shrimp if you have them, but chicken and chorizo sausage are the main ingredients for this dish.

INGREDIENTS

Serves 4

1 chicken, 2^1/2 pounds
1^1/2 onions
1 bay leaf
4 black peppercorns
1 parsley sprig
2 tablespoons vegetable oil
2 garlic cloves, chopped
1 green bell pepper, seeded and chopped
1 stalk celery, chopped
1^1/4 cups long-grain rice
1 cup chorizo sausage, sliced
1 cup chopped cooked ham
14-ounce can chopped tomatoes
    with herbs
^{1}/2 teaspoon ground chilies
^{1}/2 teaspoon cumin seeds
^{1}/2 teaspoon ground cumin
1 teaspoon dried thyme
1 cup cooked peeled shrimp
dash of Tabasco sauce
chopped parsley, to garnish

1 Place the chicken in a large flameproof casserole and add 2^1/2 cups cold water. Add the half onion, the bay leaf, peppercorns and parsley and bring to a boil. Cover and simmer gently for about 1^1/2 hours.

2 When the chicken is cooked, lift it out of the stock, remove the skin and carcass and chop the meat. Strain the stock, allow to cool and reserve.

3 Chop the remaining onion and heat the oil in a large frying pan. Add the onion, garlic, green pepper and celery. Fry for about 5 minutes, then stir in the rice, coating the grains with the oil. Add the sausage, ham and reserved chopped chicken and fry for another 2–3 minutes, stirring frequently.

4 Pour in the tomatoes and 1^1/4 cups of the reserved stock and add the ground chilies, cumin and thyme. Bring to a boil, then cover and simmer gently for 20 minutes, or until the rice is tender and the liquid is absorbed.

5 Stir in the shrimp and Tabasco. Cook for another 5 minutes, then season well and serve hot, garnished with chopped parsley.

Galveston Chicken

A Texas favorite, this crisp-roasted chicken is packed with garlic.

INGREDIENTS

Serves 4

1 chicken, 3–3$^1/_2$ pounds

juice of 1 lemon

4 garlic cloves, crushed

1 tablespoon cayenne pepper

1 tablespoon paprika

1 tablespoon dried oregano

$^1/_2$ teaspoon coarse black pepper

2 teaspoons olive oil

1 teaspoon salt

1 With a sharp knife or poultry shears, remove the backbone from the chicken. Turn it breast side up. With the heel of your hand, press down to break the breastbone, and open the chicken flat like a book. Insert a skewer through the chicken, at the thighs, to keep it flat during cooking.

2 Place the chicken in a shallow dish and pour on the lemon juice to coat.

3 In a small bowl, combine the garlic, cayenne, paprika, oregano, pepper and oil. Mix well. Rub evenly over the surface of the chicken.

4 Cover and let marinate 2–3 hours at room temperature, or chill overnight (return to room temperature before roasting).

5 Season the chicken with salt on both sides. Transfer it to a shallow roasting pan.

6 Put the pan in a cold oven and set the temperature to 400°F. Roast until the chicken is done, about 1 hour, turning occasionally and basting with the pan juices. To test, prick with a skewer: the juices should be clear.

COOK'S TIP

Roasting chicken in an oven that has not been preheated produces an especially crispy skin.

Indian Spiced Chicken

These tender marinated chicken pieces can be served hot or cold.

INGREDIENTS

Serves 4

1 chicken, 4–4¹/₂ pounds
mixed salad leaves, such as frisée and
    oakleaf lettuce or radicchio, to serve

For the marinade
²/₃ cup plain low-fat yogurt
1 teaspoon paprika
2 teaspoons grated fresh ginger
1 garlic clove, crushed
2 teaspoons garam masala
¹/₂ teaspoon salt
red food coloring (optional)
juice of 1 lemon

1 Cut the chicken into 8 pieces, using a sharp knife.

2 Combine all the marinade ingredients in a large non-reactive dish, add the chicken pieces to coat and chill for 4 hours or overnight, to allow the flavors to penetrate the meat.

3 Preheat the oven to 400°F. Remove the chicken pieces from the marinade and arrange them in a single layer in a large ovenproof dish. Bake for 30–40 minutes, or until tender. Reserve the marinade.

4 Baste with a little of the marinade while cooking. Arrange on a bed of salad leaves and serve hot or cold.

Chili Chicken

Serve as a simple supper dish with boiled potatoes and broccoli, or as a party dish with rice.

Serves 4

12 chicken thighs

1 tablespoon olive oil

1 onion, thinly sliced

1 garlic clove, crushed

1 teaspoon ground chilies or 1 dried red
chili, chopped

14-ounce can chopped tomatoes,
with their juice

1 teaspoon sugar

15-ounce can kidney beans, drained

salt and black pepper

1 Cut the chicken into large cubes, removing all skin and bones. Heat the oil in a large flameproof casserole and brown the chicken pieces on all sides. Remove with a slotted spoon and keep warm.

2 Add the onion and garlic to the casserole and cook gently until soft. Stir in the ground chilies or chopped dried chili and cook for 2 minutes. Add the tomatoes with their juice, seasoning and sugar. Bring to a boil.

3 Replace the chicken pieces, cover the casserole and simmer for about 30 minutes, until tender.

4 Add the kidney beans and gently cook for another 5 minutes to heat them through before serving.

Red-hot Chicken

*A good party dish. The chicken is
marinated the night before, so all
you have to do on the day is to cook
it in a very hot oven and serve with
wedges of lemon and a green salad.*

INGREDIENTS

Serves 4

1 chicken, 4–4^1/$_2$ pounds, cut into
   8 pieces

juice of 1 large lemon

^{2}/$_3$ cup plain low-fat yogurt

3 garlic cloves, crushed

2 tablespoons olive oil

1 teaspoon ground turmeric

2 teaspoons paprika

1 teaspoon grated fresh ginger or

   ^{1}/$_2$ teaspoon ground ginger

2 teaspoons garam masala

1 teaspoon salt

a few drops red food coloring (optional)

3 Combine the remaining
ingredients and pour the sauce
over the chicken pieces, turning
them to coat thoroughly. Cover
with plastic wrap and chill
overnight.

4 Preheat the oven to 425°F.
Remove the chicken from the
marinade and arrange in a single
layer on a baking sheet. Bake for
15 minutes, turn over, and cook
for another 15 minutes, or
until tender.

1 Skin the chicken pieces and cut
two slits in each piece.

2 Arrange them in a single layer
in a glass or ceramic dish and
pour the lemon juice over them.

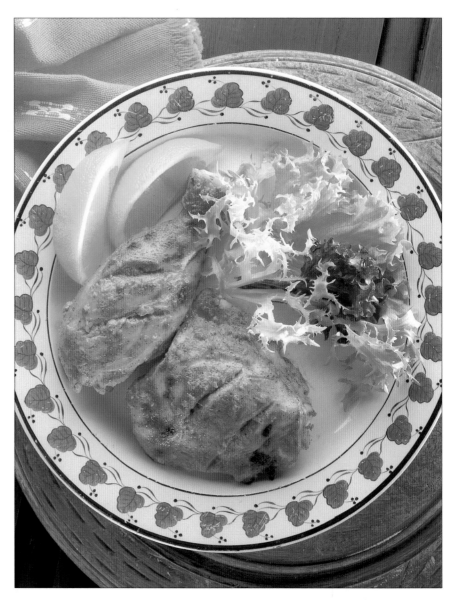

Chinese Chicken Wings

These are best eaten with fingers as an appetizer. Make sure you provide finger bowls and plenty of paper napkins; things could get messy.

INGREDIENTS

Serves 4

12 chicken wings

3 garlic cloves, crushed

$1^1/_2$-inch piece fresh ginger, grated

juice of 1 large lemon

3 tablespoons soy sauce

3 tablespoons honey

$^1/_2$ teaspoon ground chilies

$^2/_3$ cup chicken stock

salt and black pepper

lemon wedges, to garnish

3 Preheat the oven to 425°F. Remove the wings from the marinade and arrange in a single layer in a roasting pan. Bake for 20–25 minutes, basting at least twice with the marinade during cooking.

4 Place the wings on a serving plate. Add the stock to the marinade in the roasting pan, and bring to a boil. Cook to a syrupy consistency and spoon a little over the wings. Serve garnished with lemon wedges.

1 Remove the wing tips and use to make the stock. Cut the wings into two pieces.

2 Combine the remaining ingredients, except for the stock, and coat the chicken pieces in the mixture. Cover with plastic wrap and marinate overnight.

Moroccan Spiced Roast Rock Cornish Hens

Half Rock Cornish game hens served with an apricot and rice stuffing.

INGREDIENTS

Serves 4

generous 1 cup cooked long-grain rice

1 small onion, chopped finely

finely grated rind and juice of 1 lemon

2 tablespoons chopped mint

3 tablespoons chopped dried apricots

2 tablespoons plain yogurt

2 teaspoons ground turmeric

2 teaspoons ground cumin

2 Rock Cornish hens, 1 pound each

salt and black pepper

lemon slices and mint sprigs, to garnish

1 Preheat the oven to 400°F. Combine the rice, onion, lemon rind, mint and apricots. Stir in half each of the lemon juice, yogurt, turmeric, cumin, and salt and pepper.

2 Stuff the birds with the rice mixture at the neck end only. Any spare stuffing can be cooked separately. Place the birds on a rack in a roasting pan.

3 Mix together the remaining lemon juice, yogurt, turmeric and cumin, then brush over the birds. Cover loosely with foil and cook the birds in the oven for 30 minutes.

4 Remove the foil and roast for another 15 minutes, or until golden brown and the juices run clear, not pink, when pierced.

5 Cut the birds in half with a sharp knife or poultry shears, and serve with the spare rice. Garnish with lemon slices and fresh mint sprigs.

Sticky Ginger Chicken

The sweet glaze turns dark and sticky under the broiler or grill.

INGREDIENTS

Serves 4

2 tablespoons lemon juice

2 tablespoons brown sugar

1 teaspoon grated fresh ginger

2 teaspoons soy sauce

8 chicken drumsticks, skinned

black pepper

lettuce and crusty bread, to serve

1 Combine the lemon juice, brown sugar, grated ginger, soy sauce and pepper.

2 With a sharp knife, slash the chicken drumsticks about three times through the thickest part, then toss the chicken in the glaze.

3 Cook the chicken drumsticks under a hot broiler or on a barbecue grill, turning occasionally and brushing with the glaze, until the chicken is dark gold and the juices run clear, not pink, when pierced with a skewer. Serve on a bed of lettuce with crusty bread, if you like.

Butterflied Deviled Game Hens

Butterfly *describes very well the idea, if not the actual shape of birds that are split and skewered flat for cooking.*

INGREDIENTS

Serves 4

1 tablespoon powdered English mustard

1 tablespoon paprika

1 tablespoon ground cumin

4 teaspoons ketchup

1 tablespoon lemon juice

5 tablespoons butter, melted

4 Rock Cornish hens, about 1 pound each

salt

1 Combine the mustard, paprika, cumin, ketchup, lemon juice and salt until smooth, then gradually stir in the butter.

2 Using game shears or strong kitchen scissors, split each bird along one side of the backbone, then cut down the other side of the backbone to remove it.

3 Open out a bird, skin side up, then press down firmly with the heel of your hand. Pass a long skewer through one leg and out through the other to secure the bird open and flat. Repeat with the remaining birds.

4 Spread the mustard mixture evenly over the skin of the birds. Cover loosely and put in a cool place for at least 2 hours. Preheat the broiler.

5 Place the birds, skin side up, under the broiler and cook for about 12 minutes. Turn over, baste and cook for another 7 minutes, until the juices run clear.

COOK'S TIP

Butterflied game hens cook well on the barbecue grill. Make sure the coals are hot, then cook for 15–20 minutes, turning and basting frequently.

Sweet-spiced Chicken

Make sure you allow plenty of time for the chicken wings to marinate, so the flavors develop well, then use a wok or a large frying pan for stir-frying.

INGREDIENTS

Serves 4

1 fresh red chili, finely chopped

1 teaspoon ground chilies

1 teaspoon ground ginger

rind of 1 lime, finely grated

12 chicken wings

$^1/_4$ cup sunflower oil

1 tablespoon fresh cilantro, chopped

2 tablespoons soy sauce

$3^1/_2$ tablespoons honey

lime rind and fresh cilantro sprigs,
    to garnish

1 Mix the fresh chili, ground chilies, ground ginger and lime rind together. Rub the mixture into the chicken skins and let sit for at least 2 hours to allow the flavors to penetrate.

2 Heat a wok or large frying pan and add half of the oil. When the oil is hot, add half the wings and stir-fry for 10 minutes, turning frequently until crisp and golden. Drain on paper towels. Repeat with the remaining wings.

3 Add the cilantro to the hot wok and stir-fry for 30 seconds, then return the wings to the wok and stir-fry for 1 minute.

4 Stir in the soy sauce and honey, and stir-fry for 1 minute. Serve the chicken wings hot with the sauce drizzled over them, garnished with lime rind and cilantro sprigs.

Quick Chicken Curry

Curry powder can be bought in three different strengths – mild, medium and hot. Use the type you prefer to suit your taste.

INGREDIENTS

Serves 4

8 chicken legs (thighs and drumsticks)

2 tablespoons vegetable oil

1 onion, thinly sliced

1 garlic clove, crushed

1 tablespoon curry powder

1 tablespoon all-purpose flour

1³/₄ cups homemade or canned chicken stock

1 beefsteak tomato

1 tablespoon mango chutney

1 tablespoon lemon juice

salt and black pepper

1 Cut the chicken legs in half. Heat the oil in a large flame-proof casserole and brown the chicken pieces on all sides. Remove and keep warm.

2 Add the onion and crushed garlic to the casserole and cook until soft. Add the curry powder and cook gently for 2 minutes.

3 Add the flour, and gradually blend in the chicken stock and the seasoning.

4 Bring to a boil, replace the chicken pieces, cover and simmer for 20–30 minutes, or until tender and cooked through.

5 Blanch the tomato in boiling water for 45 seconds, then run it under cold water to loosen the skin. Peel and cut into small cubes.

6 Add to the chicken, with the mango chutney and lemon juice. Heat through gently and adjust the seasoning to taste.

Chicken in Green Almond Sauce

This casserole with its spicy sauce originated in Mexico.

INGREDIENTS

Serves 6

1 chicken, 3–3¹/₂ pounds, cut into
   serving pieces

2 cups homemade or canned
   chicken stock

1 onion, chopped

1 garlic clove, chopped

2 cups coarsely chopped fresh cilantro

1 green bell pepper, seeded and chopped

1 *jalapeño* pepper, seeded and chopped

10-ounce can tomatillos (Mexican green
   tomatoes)

1 cup ground almonds

2 tablespoons corn oil

salt

fresh cilantro sprig, to garnish

rice, to serve

1 Put the chicken pieces in a flameproof casserole or shallow pan. Pour in the stock, bring to a simmer, cover and cook for about 45 minutes, until tender. Drain the stock into a measuring cup and set aside.

2 Put the onion, garlic, cilantro, green and *jalapeño* peppers, tomatillos with their juice, and the almonds in a food processor. Purée fairly coarsely.

3 Heat the oil in a frying pan, add the almond mixture and cook over low heat, stirring with a wooden spoon, for 3–4 minutes. Scrape into the casserole or pan with the chicken.

4 If necessary, add water to the stock to make 2 cups. Stir it into the casserole or pan. Mix gently and simmer just long enough to blend the flavors and heat the chicken pieces through. Add salt to taste. Serve immediately, garnished with cilantro and accompanied by rice.

COOK'S TIP

If the color of the sauce seems a little pale, add 2–3 outer leaves of dark green Romaine lettuce. Cut out the central vein, chop the leaves and add at step 2.

Chicken Bobotie

Perfect for a buffet party, this mild curry dish is set with savory custard, which makes serving easy. Serve with boiled rice and chutney.

INGREDIENTS

Serves 8

two thick slices white bread

1³/4 cups milk

2 tablespoons olive oil

2 medium onions, finely chopped

3 tablespoons medium curry powder

2¹/2 pounds ground chicken

1 tablespoon apricot jam, chutney or
    sugar

2 tablespoons wine vinegar or lemon juice

3 large eggs, beaten

¹/3 cup dark or golden raisins

12 whole almonds

salt and black pepper

3 Mash the bread in the milk and add to the pan with one of the beaten eggs and the raisins.

4 Grease a 6-cup shallow ovenproof dish with butter. Spoon in the chicken mixture and level the top. Cover with buttered foil and bake in the oven for 30 minutes.

5 Meanwhile, beat the remaining eggs and milk. Remove the dish from the oven and lower the temperature to 300°F. Break up the meat using a fork and pour the egg mixture on top.

6 Scatter on the almonds and bake, uncovered, for 30 minutes until set and brown.

1 Preheat the oven to 350°F. Soak the bread in ²/3 cup of the milk. Heat the oil in a frying pan and gently fry the onions until tender then add the curry powder and cook for another 2 minutes.

2 Add the ground chicken and brown all over, separating the grains of meat as they brown. Remove from the heat and season with salt and black pepper. Add the apricot jam, chutney or sugar and the wine vinegar or lemon juice.

Chicken Biryani

A deceptively easy curry to make,
and very tasty, too.

Serves 4

1$\frac{1}{2}$ cups basmati rice, rinsed

$\frac{1}{2}$ teaspoon salt

5 whole cardamom pods

2–3 whole cloves

1 cinnamon stick

3 tablespoons vegetable oil

3 onions, sliced

4 chicken breasts, 6 ounces each, cubed,
  skinned and boned

$\frac{1}{4}$ teaspoon ground cloves

5 cardamom pods, seeds removed and
  ground

$\frac{1}{4}$ teaspoon ground chilies

1 teaspoon ground cumin

1 teaspoon ground coriander

$\frac{1}{2}$ teaspoon black pepper

3 garlic cloves, finely chopped

1 teaspoon finely chopped fresh ginger

juice of 1 lemon

4 tomatoes, sliced

2 tablespoons chopped fresh cilantro

$\frac{2}{3}$ cup plain yogurt

$\frac{1}{2}$ teaspoon saffron strands soaked in
  2 teaspoons hot milk

3 tablespoons toasted slivered almonds
  and fresh cilantro sprigs, to garnish

plain yogurt, to serve

1 Preheat the oven to 375°F.
Bring a pan of water to a boil
and add the rice, salt, cardamom
pods, cloves and cinnamon stick.
Boil for 2 minutes and then drain,
leaving the whole spices in the rice.

2 Heat the oil in a pan and fry
the onions for 8 minutes, until
browned. Add the chicken
followed by all the ground spices,
the garlic, ginger and lemon juice.
Stir-fry for 5 minutes.

3 Transfer the chicken mixture
to a casserole and lay the sliced
tomatoes on top. Sprinkle on the
cilantro, spoon on the plain yogurt
and top with the drained rice.

4 Drizzle the saffron and milk
over the rice and pour on
$\frac{2}{3}$ cup of water.

5 Cover tightly and bake in the
oven for 1 hour. Transfer to a
warmed serving platter and
remove the whole spices from the
rice. Garnish with toasted almonds
and cilantro and serve with extra
plain yogurt.

Index